Su
Hawaii

Judi Thompson

Preface by Katharine Luomala, Ph.D.

Schiffer Publishing Ltd

4880 Lower Valley Road, Atglen, Pennsylvania 19310

Cover Photo: Tiki In Hawaii @ Alan Crosthwaite. Image from BigStockPhotos.com

Following photos are from BigStockPhoto.com. Volcanic Lava 1 © Robert Pack. The Ocean Viewed Over Lava Rock In Hawaii © Steven Austin. Green Leaves © Dewayne Flowers. 3 Skulls © David Wood. Lava Rock © Debbie Smith.

Other Schiffer Books on Related Subjects:

Hawaiian Fish, 0-7643-2139-0, $14.99
Hawaii Remembered: Postcards from Paradise, 0-7643-2219-2, $24.95
Hauntings in Florida's Panhandle, 978-0-7643-3134-3, $14.99

Schiffer Books are available at special discounts for bulk purchases for sales promotions or premiums. Special editions, including personalized covers, corporate imprints, and excerpts can be created in large quantities for special needs. For more information contact the publisher:

Schiffer Publishing Ltd.
4880 Lower Valley Road
Atglen, PA 19310
Phone: (610) 593-1777; Fax: (610) 593-2002
E-mail: Info@schifferbooks.com

For the largest selection of fine reference books on this and related subjects, please visit our web site at **www.schifferbooks.com.**
We are always looking for people to write books on new and related subjects. If you have an idea for a book please contact us at the above address.

This book may be purchased from the publisher. Include $5.00 for shipping. Please try your bookstore first. You may write for a free catalog.

In Europe, Schiffer books are distributed by:

Bushwood Books
6 Marksbury Ave.
Kew Gardens
Surrey TW9 4JF England
Phone: 44 (0) 20 8392-8585; Fax: 44 (0) 20 8392-9876
E-mail: info@bushwoodbooks.co.uk
Website: www.bushwoodbooks.co.uk
Free postage in the U.K., Europe; air mail at cost.

Copyright © 2009 by Judi Thompson
Library of Congress Control Number: 2008939451

Designed by Stephanie Daugherty
Type set in MatrixScriptBoldLining/NewsGoth BT

ISBN: 978-0-7643-3186-2
Printed in United States of America

Dedication

For Rebecca Jean Thompson,
who accompanied me in this adventure

Contents

Epigraph 7

Preface... 8

Introduction.. 10

Part I: Haunted Hawaii 12

Chokeneck! ☠ The Co-ed and the Haunted Dorm ☠ Echoes from the Arizona ☠ A Ghostly Hitchhiker ☠ A Haunted Hollywood Hideaway ☠ The Phantom in the Field ☠ The Ghostly Voyeur ☠ The Haunted Mansion ☠ Plantation Ghost Tales ☠ Blue Lights of Saddle Road ☠ The Sitting Ghost of Mauna Kea ☠ The Pig Hunt ☠ The White Lady of Kaanapali ☠ Ulum Bala: Feast of the Hungry Ghosts ☠ The Demons in the Field ☠ The Nature Spirits of Waiahole Valley ☠ The Haunted Barge ☠ A Haunted Coffee Shack at Keauhou ☠ Night Visitors ☠ The Ghost in the Nursery ☠ A Brush with Pele ☠ A Ghost at Puna

Part II: Kupuna Make A'ole Loa (Hawaii's Elders Never Die) 82

Introduction... 82

Inez Ashdown Remembers 86

Early Days in Wyoming ☠ We Come to Hawaii ☠ I Meet the Captain in his Tomb ☠ Memories of Queen Liliuokalani ☠ An Amakua for our Family ☠ Pele and the Ranch at Hamakua ☠ The Haunted Cane ☠ Lahaina Then

Stories of Rubelite Johnson's Family 103

Uncle Lono and the Blue Lights ☠ Ekikela Comes Back ☠ The Ghost Dog of Poipu ☠ the Three Skulls of Lahaulipua ☠ Wahine of the Stone ☠ Rachel Moki and the Black Pig

Auntie Harriet Ne of Molokai 116
    A Tale of Night Marchers ☠ the Missing Girl and the Mu People
    ☠ I Meet the Menehune

The Great Storyteller Richard Marks & Friends 125
    Kalaupapa Talk Story ☠ Ghost Lover ☠ The Legend of the L'iang
    L'iang Tree ☠ The Haunted Lighthouse

June Gutmanis' Ghosties 151
    The Ghost in the Tri-Corner Hat ☠ Shaseda ☠ Ghost Riders ☠
    A Little Night Music ☠ Ghost Dogs

Collectable Tales 160
    Katharine Luomala Shares ☠ The Skeleton in the Cave ☠
    The Ghosts of Mana ☠ The Invisible Hand ☠ The Story of Napoleon
    Kaloii Kapukuui

Part III: Firehouse Ghost Tales **167**

Introduction 167

Wylie Station #25 170
    Chokeneck ☠ Fire! ☠ Apparitions in the Apparatus Room

Kakaako Station (Downtown Honolulu) 179
    Shadow Man ☠ The Blessing of the Crooked Wall ☠ The Pig Stealer
    ☠ The Face on the Wall ☠ Menehune Walk ☠ The Ghost Who Threw
    Stones ☠ Kahuna 'Ana'Ana ☠ The Bad Luck Lava Rock

Makiki Station 197
    Talk Story Under a Full Moon

Makoana Station 201
    The Ghost Upstairs

Fireboat Station (Honolulu Harbor) 205
    Aulele ☠ The Headless Woman ☠ Premonition of a Disaster

Part IV: What IS a Ghost **210**

A Spirited Conversation with Charles Kenn 210

Epigraph: Ghost Drummer

*I*t was the summer of 1941, just before World War II. My aunt had flown to Kauai on holiday. It was her first trip to that island and she had journeyed to the famous groves of the Coco Palms Hotel. On one side of the grounds lay the royal birthing stones; on the other, *Ho'o Heiau,* a sacred place. At that time there was a grass hut erected in the old style on the side of the hill leading to the *heiau.* An ancient drum, a *pahu*, rested in the hut.

My aunt meandered up the path and entered the hut. The inside was deep in shadow and the air smelled musty. There were no trade winds and the air was still. A single ray of sunshine piercing the gloom threw a jagged slice of light across the face of the drum, as the huge *pahu* loomed with a tangible presence of its own, silent with the weight of time.

My aunt lightly ran her fingers across the scarred surface of the *pahu* and imagined the holy ceremonies long gone in which it had played its part. Suddenly she abruptly turned away and stepped from the dark hut into the topical brilliance of the Hawaiian sunlight. She wanted to see the bell stone on the top of the hill and began to walk up the path to the *heiau.*

She had taken but a few steps when she heard it, muffled yet distinct. The drum was beating. There was no one there. Only the drum...

Rubelite Johnson, Ph.D.

Preface

A seeing eye, a listening ear, a nurtured belief, and a marveling imagination characterize these residents of the Hawaiian Islands who so sincerely and earnestly tell of their inexplicable experiences that they attribute to supernatural beings and forces. After the first thrill of fear and excitement has passed, the disbelief of any skeptical listeners is likely to fade when they too, on a lonely beach at night or on a forested mountain trail, hear drums and marching feet and see shadows floating toward them—or they awaken in the night choking as if a phantom has them by the throat. Their rational explanations no longer satisfy and they say, "I never believed what the old folks used to say about these things, but now I know!" The puzzling events take place not only at home or on a beach or mountain trail, but also in a firehouse, a hotel, and a college dormitory or even near the sunken *Arizona* and *Utah* at Pearl Harbor.

Judi Thompson has selected here only a few of the numerous accounts she has gathered from people with first-hand experiences that include encounters with (to name a few) ghosts of people or white dogs, mysterious "little people" like the Menehune and the Mu, and friendly family sharks who are transformed stillborn infants. The stories, which come both from Hawaiians and other ethnic groups in the Islands, sometimes mingle internationally known beliefs into new combinations.

Certain collections included in this book are of particular note. One is a series of stories from fire stations and the fireboat at Honolulu. Then, Mary Kawena Pukui and Inez Ashdown, well-known specialists on Hawaiiana, provide autobiographical

narratives that enrich our knowledge of their remarkable lives and of the geographical and cultural milieu of the Islands during the nineteenth and twentieth centuries. These experts are unsurpassed in frankness and skill when they "talk story" about their experiences.

Katharine Luomala, Ph.D.,
Honolulu, Hawaii

Dr. Katharine Luomala, author of *HULA KI'I: Hawaiian Puppetry*, with Judi Thompson at the Polynesian Cultural Center, Laie.

Introduction

Supernatural Hawaii began as an assignment. In 1984, I was working as executive editor for The Institute for Polynesian Studies when the idea for a new title in our series Pamphlets Polynesia was broached: a folklore project, "Firehouse Ghost Tales." Our senior editor, a noted folklorist from the mainland, cautioned me that it would always be second or third-hand experiences, as folklore tends to be hair-raising tales that always happened to "a friend" or "my brother's aunt" or "my cousin's neighbor." I remember thinking, "Hmm, I don't know about that. This is Hawaii." Forewarned, I enlisted my daughter, Rebecca, a senior at Punahou, and we set out one dark moonless night to interview the firemen of Nuuanu Station. Little did we know what was in store for us!

Jan Yasuda, the first fireman we interviewed, exclaimed, "Chokeneck? That happened to me!" And our innocuous little project jumped from folklore to first-person experiential data into parapsychology in one leap. The stories we gathered became more fascinating as we progressed and almost all of it was first-hand, personal experiences. When I had enough material, I presented it to the head of the Institute. He was impressed, but gently explained that the booklet I was proposing "went way beyond folklore" and was unsuitable for IPS. He acknowledged the importance of the project, however, and suggested that I continue to pursue it on my own. I did.

What followed over the next four years was a series of oral history interviews conducted throughout the Hawaiian Islands with people of all backgrounds, nationalities, religions, belief systems, and cultures. Some names were well known, some not. What emerged was a collection of human experience that naturally fell into classic folklore motifs, and clearly established itself as universal. Whether I took my tape recorder into unusual places, such as the leper colony on Molokai, or met with people in usual places such as coffee shops, one thing became clear: they were telling their truth as they had experienced it.

Supernatural Hawaii is the result. The stories, while lightly edited, are presented in the voice of the storyteller, their words unchanged.

Shortly before I left my job as editor to complete this book, I was sitting at my desk in the cubical that was my office stealing a few moments to review notes and material for the project. Suddenly, the girl in the next office called out, "Judi, are you all right?" I replied that I was fine. She appeared in the doorway with her eyes as big as saucers. "I just saw a big cloud of smoke drift up from your desk and out the window!" she gasped. "It looked like a great cloud of mist or cigarette smoke. I knew it couldn't be that because you don't smoke and smoking is not allowed in the building anyway as it would have set off the smoke detectors!"

I could only assume that I had had a ghostly visitor checking up on my work!

As this book has been many years in the making, many of the participants—elderly when interviewed—have now passed on themselves, giving the manuscript an even greater poignancy and importance. I invite you to accompany me as I relive these fascinating visits.

Judi Thompson
Pepeekeo, Hamakua Coast, Hawaii

1

Haunted Hawaii

Chokeneck!

Ken Coffey is head of the Graphics Art Center at the Polynesian Cultural Center, Laie, Hawaii. He is also a professional painter, sculptor, illustrator, printmaker, woodcarver, and photographer.

*I*t happened to me right here on campus (Brigham Young University). My wife and I were living in the married students housing. One morning I woke up and saw the sun shining through the window on the wall of the bedroom. My wife was asleep beside me. At first, I heard noises in the kitchen when I knew nobody was there. Then I suddenly felt this weight pressing me down on the bed and I realized that I couldn't move any part of my body except my eyes. I couldn't see anything there. I tried to cry out to my wife, but I couldn't make noises—nothing would come out. My wife never woke up. I wasn't scared because somehow I knew it wasn't a permanent condition and that it would pass. In fact, I was almost curious as to what parts of me I was able to move. I found I could move my little finger and that was all. I couldn't see anyone, there was no figure, but I *felt* as if someone were there. Finally, it just eased away and left me. When I told my wife about it, she said she didn't hear a thing.

About a year later, however, the same thing happened to her. We had moved into another apartment here in Laie. This time it happened at night. Suddenly, my wife said, she felt the weight upon her and she was unable to move or cry out. She remembered what I had told her, so she wasn't as scared as she might have been otherwise. It finally left her, but she considered it an unnerving experience.

In New Zealand, my father had many strange things happen to him. He told us these stories after I had grown up and had gone home to visit him. Some experiences happened to him when he was a boy, some when he was a young man, but as he got older, the experiences stopped. He told me about a man who walked through his door, just the shape of a figure; he was all dark. He would walk right through the door and then disappear.

One night a friend of his walked into his room, sat down in a chair, and proceeded to talk to him. He talked for a long time. Then he disappeared into thin air! My dad realized then that this man must have died and had come to say good-bye. Sure enough, the very next day he got word that the fellow had passed away.

One time when my father was small, he swore at his grandmother who raised him. She scolded him and said, "Your ghosts are going to get you for that!" Sure enough, that night a figure came into his room and pressed him to the bed. He struggled and cried out to his grandmother who was sitting in the next room with a visitor. When the man inquired about the noise, she replied, "Oh, that's just Coffey and his ghost," and she refused to lift a finger.

Author's Note: The American Folklore Society has published an excellent book on the subject: The Terror That Comes in the Night: An Experience-Centered Study of Supernatural Assault Traditions, Vol. 7, David J. Hufford, December 1, 1982.

The Co-ed and the Haunted Dorm

When I first came to Brigham Young University-Hawaii Campus from New Zealand, I was a student staying in the boy's dorm with another fellow. One night about midnight, the security guard came to us for help. He told us that there was a student on campus, a girl from New York City, who had gotten spooked—and, I tell you, SHE WAS SPOOKED.

The girl had been visiting a friend across the hall and had returned to her own room at 1 a.m. to find her roommate fast asleep. Before she went to bed, she happened to look at the door she had just shut and noticed that it was open. Thinking that her roommate (who was still in bed) must have gotten up, gone out and come back, leaving the door open, she shut it again and locked it. A few minutes later, she looked up from her bed and saw it open once more. She was starting to get annoyed, but she got up and shut it again. Sure enough, the door opened a third time and nobody was there.

She then told her roommate to "knock off opening the door," and her roommate sleepily replied that she hadn't gotten out of bed. Not wanting to see the door open again, the girl reversed her direction in bed so that her head was near the door instead of her feet. By this time, her roommate was snoring.

All of a sudden, the lights started blinking on and off and something heavy pressed her so flat to the bed that she couldn't move. Then it picked her up three feet into the air, turned her around so that she was facing the door again, and dropped her back down on the bed! Again, the door was open.

Well, she shot out of there making all kinds of noises that she had been spooked and that's when the security guard came to get us. We went over to the room, blessed it, exorcized it, and did everything that the Mormon Church taught us to do. Even so, the girl wasn't that keen to go back. She was so upset that she called her mother in New York to tell her what had happened. Her mother replied, "only superstitious natives believe in stuff like that." Boy, was that girl mad!

Echoes from the Arizona

Roxanne Faith is married to a U.S. Navy Captain stationed at Submarine Base, Pearl Harbor. She and her family lived in officers' quarters on Ford Island, which served as mooring for many ships destroyed during the Japanese attack on December 7, 1941. This interview took place at the Sub Base Officers' Club on August 13, 1984.

I had been living on Ford Island for eight years, since 1974. My husband was a pilot stationed at Pearl Harbor before he retired. We lived in magnificent old quarters, *kama'aina* style. Quarters like that just don't exist anymore. I experienced many things during the years we were there: visions, presences...whatever you want to call them. There was a presence in my house that liked to open and close doors and drink from the refrigerator. We had panels of French doors that would mysteriously open and close, but I was not in fear. I was never in fear. Often my Hawaiian friends would come over and they would sense the presences. I don't know if they were male or female, but they were spirits that somehow needed to stay, so I allowed them to stay and I let them be.

The house we lived in faced Pearl City and not the *Arizona.* The *Utah* was in my front yard. I actually heard screams and cries coming from the decks of that ship. It was December 7, 1941 all over again. I would receive sounds, smells,

The U.S. Navy conducts tours to the *Arizona Memorial* at Pearl Harbor via ferry boat. Pearl City lies in the background.

and visions as clear as if they were on a television screen. It was as if I was seeing a very clear movie, except that the movie was inside, a *seeing* with inner eyes. Sometimes it would be overpowering. I could smell the smoke and the burning flesh and I could hear the cries. It would come at night (I

The *U.S.S. Arizona Memorial* at Pearl Harbor still flies the American flag. It's considered a commissioned ship in the United States Navy as so many men are still aboard.

receive at night) and it would come on the wind when the winds would change. Usually the winds are soft and gentle, but when they come from the south, there is an unhappiness about the wind...a bitterness.

The place where the *Utah* was moored was also the scene of older tragedies and those spirits from long ago mingled with the "modern spirits," the other dead. So there were any number of sad things that have occurred on Ford Island, but there were good times too. Hawaiians would come over from Mililani in their canoes to party. The island had also been a place of healing in the past. And it was the place of the "Man with the Flowing White Beard," where Hawaiian women of ancient times would come across the water to have sexual relations with men who were very potent in order to conceive children. These were not orgies, for their only purpose was so these women could bear offspring.

I have seen over there at night big processions of Hawaiians and could hear the drums. They were all men. Night Walkers. I could see the torches, smell them...and it was as real as if it were right here. Marvelous, just marvelous.

Now I have been out to the *Arizona* many times and it is so heavy to go there. Each time I go, I have such a strong sadness of the presences that are still there that I always come away carrying these feelings with me. Sometimes I hear the clawing and scratching on the metal of the ship from the spirits of the dead trying to get out. These men were trapped during the attack on Pearl Harbor, and they are trapped there still. They were taken from their lives and their dreams and their families, and I believe, they want to get their revenge. Why that particular group of souls happened to be caught on that particular ship on December 7, I don't know, but I have heard a definite wailing and a crying and an agony. There are times in the day when I just don't want to go by there. These men are tied. They are seeking release, searching for release, praying for release, and I don't think that memorial ceremonies and strewing flowers on the water is going to release them. I think it will take more than hocus-pocus and shake and rattle.

The spirits on the *Utah* are not caught although the death and agony are still there. They have either gone away or co-mingled with the older Hawaiian spirits who have died in the water there. The men of the Arizona are trapped in their ship still. They can't come and go or live in anybody's house. They are tied.

A Ghostly Hitchhiker

Kalani Hanohano is a journalist and audio-video specialist. He's also the former managing editor for Hawaii Island Guide magazine.

I was sitting in the doctor's office for my appointment, and there was a Filipino man next to me who was obviously waiting to see the doctor too. He was in a cast and looked like he was in pretty bad shape so I asked what had happened to him. I guess he didn't want to talk about it because he responded with some kind of muffled reply and didn't really answer me. When his name was called, he went into the doctor's office and the nurse came out. I was curious so I asked the nurse, "What's the deal with the Filipino guy?"

"Oh," she said, "he got into a car accident."

"What happened?" I persisted.

"Well, we don't believe what he keeps telling us," she replied, "but apparently he is sticking to his story. It seems that he was driving down by Campbell Industrial Park to an area he was supposed to go to. It was evening. All of a sudden, he looked into his rear view mirror and there was his dead mother staring at him from the back seat of the car. It spooked him so much he ran off the side of the road and into another car. He really did himself in."

"My God!" I cried. "His own mother did that to him?"

I have heard stories of ghostly hitchhikers before. It is well known in the Islands that there was an old Hawaiian man who used to catch the bus in Waianae over and over again. He was always dressed in his best suit, the one he had been buried in. He always liked to take the same route. Everyone on the bus saw him and although all of the bus drivers knew him, it seemed to take them by surprise each time it happened. It seemed they never recognized him for who he was until he got off at the next stop. This story was written up in the *Honolulu Advertiser* a couple of years ago. There are stories of ghostly hitchhikers all over the world so it appears to be a universal phenomenon, but I didn't expect to be sitting next to one in the doctor's office.

A Haunted Hollywood Hideaway

Hannah "Nana" Veary—Hawaiian teacher, metaphysician, and spiritual healer—is the author of Change We Must. Richard Chamberlain wrote, "I met her early in my stay here, around 1979. I remember her saying, very forcefully, 'I am not a kahuna' (master). But she was. She was a spiritual master, the most wonderful woman, full of life, and she had a magical way of combining the ancient traditions of the Hawaiians with what we might call Christian beliefs... all inclusive, warm and full of love... with a supreme reverence for all forms of life, from rocks to flowers to clouds and the broader sweep of people and the environment."

The following interview was conducted on April 20, 1983 at the Yum Yum Tree in Kahala on Oahu.

Richard Chamberlain, a famous Hollywood actor, has a home here in Maile, a big house. Whenever I hold a retreat, I take people there. One day he called me after he had just returned from filming an epic movie in Japan. He had a big crew with him. He said, "Amah, we have been having some things happen in this house and I wonder if you would come to bless it for me?"

We talked about it and I agreed to come, but I said, "It will be early, five o'clock in the morning. I must bless the house before the sun comes up."

"Fine," he said, "Come any time. We will be waiting for you. Please come and spend the night."

I spent the night in the upstairs bedroom of the big beach house. Just before I woke up at 4 a.m., I heard the rocking chair at the foot of my bed creaking and squeaking as it rocked back and forth. A girl in the next bed who was sharing the room with me heard it too. She saw the chair rocking, but saw no one in it. I saw an apparition, which looked like an old sea captain smoking a pipe he held clenched in his teeth. He looked at me as he rocked.

"Who's there?" I said. As soon as I spoke, my roommate said that the chair stopped rocking; however, I saw that it continued to rock and the old man continued to look at me. "Now, what's this?" I thought. I got up and went into the bathroom to get dressed and when I came out the chair was empty.

I went downstairs to meet Richard and the others who were waiting for the blessing to begin. As I descended the stairway, I noticed that the elegant old banister was made of *koa* wood, as were the floors of the entire first level.

"Richard!" I cried, "These floors are made of *koa* wood! Where did it come from?"

"Oh," he said, "I bought this house from a missionary family up at Moanalua. It came from their old house there on the knoll by Tripler."

"Oh no!" I thought. "That's it." I didn't know this place had a connection with that family. These particular people, members of the "Big Five," were not well regarded by the old Hawaiians in the valley because of the way they had mistreated them down through the years. In fact, the Hawaiians who lived in Moanalua had cursed them. "We are long suffering now," they said, "but a time will come when your line will come to eat its own feces." That was the curse and it did come to pass. I knew the nurse who tended one of the male descendents of the family who was *pupule* (crazy) in the head and sure enough, that is exactly what happened to him one day.

At any rate, the blessing began. We went around from room to room and I blessed each part of the house. There was one bedroom on the other side of the bath from Richard's room that was full of the sleeping camera crew. When we came to that room, Richard offered to wake them up. Trying to be a "good guy," I told him to let them sleep.

"The rest of the house is blessed," I said, "that room will be covered too." Little did I know!

Some weeks later, I took several people back to the beach house at Maile for a retreat. That time I ended up sleeping in the room I had neglected to bless. All day long everything was fine, but that night things began to happen. I had gone to bed and was just falling asleep when an overnight case I had brought suddenly fell off the chair it was sitting on with a bang. I thought it strange as I was alone in the room, but I got out of bed, picked up the case, and replaced it on the chair. I went back to bed and in a few minutes, BANG, off it went again. I got up once more and put it back on the chair. This time I pushed it way back so it couldn't possibly fall off again. I returned to bed and not a moment had passed when BANG, down it went on the floor again.

"What's this?" I said.

Then I heard a voice, laughing. In Hawaiian, it said, "You thought you got rid of us, but you only sent us all in here!"

The spirits in the house had simply retreated to the one unblessed room with the sleeping people! I found out later that everyone who had slept in that room since the blessing had been similarly bothered.

I am seventy years old. My mother was from Pearl City Peninsula. She was born and raised there and she was the "caretaker" of Ka'ahupahau, a fishing *heiau* (altar) dedicated to the shark god, Ka'ahupahau. When the fishermen brought in their catch, the first canoe was always piled full of fish and brought into the shore to the *heiau* as a kind of tithing to the gods. The rest of the catch was divided up among the fishermen. There was one special canoe that was reserved for Ka'ahupahau. When it was brought back, my mother would get in and paddle over to the Navy docking at Pearl Harbor. Of course, this was before the U.S. Navy built their base there. The shark lived down under that spot. Sometimes he would swim up to the canoe and sometimes he would stay down. When he stayed down, my mother would dive over into the water and swim below to where he was. Sometimes she would get on his back and ride him back up to the surface, where she would feed him the fish from the canoe. He was almost like a pet. Then when he was through eating, she would sometimes put a rope in his mouth and he would pull her through the water. At times she would get on his back and ride him like a dolphin back to the shore.

Later when the Navy moved in to build Pearl Harbor Naval Base, they had all kinds of trouble when they tried to build on that site. Many people were killed in accidents time and time again. The Hawaiians warned them that the area was *kapu* (taboo) to Ka'ahupahau, but they didn't listen. After they lost a few more people, they decided that perhaps the Hawaiians were worth listening to and asked my mother if she would come to bless the site. She said no, she did not want to do that, so they asked a Hawaiian man to come. He did bless the site and had *luau* (traditional Hawaiian feast) and all of that. From that time on, it was all right

Author's note: This blessing is well documented by the U.S. Navy. The story is included in their official tour of Pearl Harbor.

The Phantom in the Field

A potter and craftsman, Mark Kadota was a neighbor of June Gutmanis living in Waianae on the North Shore.

It was real strange. There was a group of us living in Waianae Valley back in 1975: Marie, Hugh, Larry, Sukie, and me. Three other friends had found the place first. They were teachers living down the road with twenty-two other people and they needed space. When they found this place it was a chicken house; a shack with no doors and chicken shit all over the place. They decided to clean it up so they scrubbed, nailed down carpet, put up a door, got a water tank, and made it livable. They had been there for a year and then we moved in.

I wasn't frightened to be in the valley then. It was beautiful and I would walk through the hills alone and didn't think a thing about it. There was a main house where the landlady and her husband lived, a garden, and stream on two acres of land. Further down the stream at the edge of a great grey field was a ceramic studio and a geodesic dome. That's where I lived, in the dome. Across the stream by the edge of the field was a little sugar shack where the landlady sewed at night.

One night as I was walking back to my dome, I heard the landlady sewing in her place. The next morning she demanded to know if we had been playing tricks on her during the night. She said that she heard the door open with a creaking sound, but when she looked, the door remained closed and locked. Her dog, Winter, began barking like crazy and all his fur was standing up. Then she heard a woman sighing. Of course, we hadn't been playing tricks on her. Why would we do that?

"Oh, it must be the spirit again," she said matter-of-factly. "There is a ghost that comes and she doesn't like women. She likes men."

She went on to tell us that every time she had a fight with her husband, the ghost would "do something" to her. One night she locked Joe out of the house and yelled that she wasn't going to sleep with him. No sooner had she climbed into bed than the sheets were ripped off. Another time, she and Joe had an argument just before he left on a trip. That night after she went to bed, not only were the sheets ripped off but a square plate from the ceiling fell right next to her head missing her by inches.

When she and Joe had yet another fight, a two-by-four flew at her foot out of nowhere. If it had hit her, she said, it surely would have broken a bone.

"So I think the ghost likes men and not women," she concluded. "She always takes his side."

Joe knew about the ghost. "Don't have this place blessed," he declared. "I like her."

It wasn't long after this conversation that I began having a series of vivid dreams. These dreams were extremely clear and I would wake up at night remembering every detail. I dreamt about a woman. She had long black hair, but she would never show herself so I couldn't see her face. At first she would always be behind me. "I am here," she said. "You needn't be afraid of me."

In a second dream, she told me she had died violently and her life had been unfulfilled. I felt she wanted something as she said there was something she had come back to complete. She also said that she belonged to the land. I thought these dreams were strange, but I classified them as just dreams.

One day, however, I was working in the garden by the field picking peas. The sun had set, it was twilight and almost dark when I suddenly heard a crackling in the bushes. I felt as if someone were there watching me. It was far into the valley and I knew nobody was around. I was all by myself in the garden and yet I felt a definite presence. I broke out in goose bumps and told myself how silly I was being. I began to walk back to the house, but kept hearing something behind as if I were being followed. When I looked around, nothing was there.

When I got home, Marie and Hugh were there with some other people. I told them that I felt somebody had been following me and the words were no sooner out of my mouth when I turned and saw a shadow go by the window. Even then, I didn't think too much of it.

I continued to have the dreams. I dreamt about the same woman and each time she would tell me a little more about herself in bits and snatches, here and there. One night I was potting in the dome. It was a no-moon night, pitch black and creepy still. Suddenly a wind started up, a low wind that seemed to be centered in different areas. Again I had the definite feeling that someone was watching me. There were tiny low windows all around the dome and I felt as if someone was going from window to window looking in. I told myself to stop it. My imagination was really working overtime and I should not feed it energy, right? So I started putting things away and yet I felt as though I were being watched.

All of a sudden, I broke out in chicken skin as I saw something move out of the corner of my eye. I looked up just as the figure of a woman floated past the door. She looked as if she were made up of lines, like a static generator when it goes zzzzzap. It was as if she was made up of electricity or silvery-white lightening. Her movements were smooth as she drifted by the door and she looked right in at me. She was normal sized, just like she was there and she was complete, but she didn't look solid. She appeared as if you could stick your hand right through her, but she was made up of *something.* She looked as though she were made of light. If you photographed her, I think it would be fuzzy as though the light would blend out of her but be contained within her at the same time. Does that make sense? The door was small and you had to crouch to enter. She looked as though she were bending over as she floated by to get a look at me. It must have been a matter of seconds and I heard nothing but the wind. Just the wind.

At this point I freaked. Finally I found a lantern and literally flew back to the house and I felt she was behind me all the way.

The next morning my landlady said, "Oh by the way, I saw the ghost last night."

"You did!" I yelped.

"Yes," she continued, "the dogs were barking so I looked outside and I saw her float across the yard."

When I asked what she looked like, she replied that it was the form of a woman, but it looked as if it were made up of a lot of electrical lines. Her description exactly matched what I had seen. Where I described her as "drifting along," my landlady described her as "floating along."

I told her what I had experienced the night before and she said, "Oh, you've met her of course. She is here."

Now up to this point, we had led a laid-back kind of life in the valley and we thought the ghost didn't really exist. We began to talk about her now. We felt she came from the field.

Two strange events seemed to herald the next chapter. A large white owl began flying back and forth over and over again and Sukie's owl that had disappeared over a year before suddenly reappeared...*from the field*.

One night the ghost appeared in my dream again. Her long black hair was over her face and she was crying, "I'm so sad, I'm so sad," over and over again. I knew she was crying because I rejected her.

"Go away!" I kept thinking. "I don't want anything to do with you."

The next morning I was home alone with Hugh, who was my lover at that time. Marie and Larry were rehearsing a play somewhere, and Sukie had split, saying, "The ghost doesn't want a strong body, she wants a weak body and it's me. I'm not coming back until the ghost is gone!" So Hugh and I were by ourselves.

Suddenly we got into an intense fight. There was no basis for it at all. It was vicious name-calling for no reason. We had fought before, but it had always been relevant. This was abstract fighting. At one point, Hugh put his head down and started moaning, "I'm so sad, I'm so sad..."

I looked at him and thought, "This is exactly what I saw in my dream last night."

Then he said, "I think I'll go out in the field."

"No, don't go out in the field!" I yelled. "We have to get out of here right now!"

That night Hugh and I decided not to go back to the dome and we all slept in the living room of the main house, except for Larry who was in the main bedroom by himself.

"I don't know why you are all so freaked out about the ghost," he said. "I wouldn't mind if she contacted me. I wonder how she died?"

"Fine, Larry, she can contact you," I said. "It's scaring me. I don't know how she died and I don't care."

Larry went into his room and the rest of us watched television for awhile. Finally it was time to go to sleep so we bedded down in the living room. The dogs were whimpering nervously. Suddenly a wind came up and howled around the building. It sounded as though rocks were being thrown at the walls. It was an intense night.

Suddenly a cat let out a blood-curdling screech and ripped through Larry's bedroom screen jumping onto his throat and digging its claws into his chest. Larry leaped up screaming, "She's here! She's here!" and ran out of the bedroom white as a sheet.

We all jumped up to turn on the lights. When we ran into the bedroom, the screen was ripped. Larry told us that he had had a nightmare. There was no sign of the cat.

Larry told me he had a nightmare where a group of men were leading a woman across the field to a tree where they were going to hang her. It was such an ugly dream that he pushed the whole scene from his mind. It was at this point that the cat had come flying through the window. Just as this happened, he saw her hung in his dream.

That same night Marie got choked. She had bedded down in the living room with the rest of us and her head was hanging off the couch when something abruptly woke her.

She felt a great heaviness and a sense of a presence. She said she was awake, but her eyes were still closed and she was unable to open them. Her throat seemed paralyzed so she was unable to call out. She felt hands around her throat that seemed very strong while at the same time she felt the pressure of someone sitting on her. She could move the lower half of her body, but not the top. It was at that moment that Larry came running in screaming and it all instantly disappeared as though it had been released. Marie said later that she thought it might be the ghost attacking her thinking she was *my* girlfriend—which was certainly not the case.

The next morning we decided to have the house blessed. We would stay with friends until the priest could come. The odd thing was that once we decided to leave, it seemed to take hours to actually go. It took from eight in the morning to noon just to get out toothbrushes and towels. I would say, "Does anybody want any water?" Then I would light a cigarette and start talking about something else. Then I would say, "Oh, the water. I'll go get it," but then I would say to someone, "Where did you get those pants?" We were spaced out, wandering aimlessly in slow motion. We wanted to leave, we were going to leave, but it was as if she kept coming into our minds to detain us because she didn't want us to go. It was as if a magnetic force was holding us there. Finally we said we were not going to talk about it, we were not going to write a list about it, we were just going to leave. It was past four when we got our stuff and walked out the door.

By this time it was almost dusk. In order to get to the parking lot, we had to walk through some bushes and trees and... *this* is the eeriest part of it all. There was no wind. It was very still, but each bush we passed bent over as though brushed by an invisible presence with a swishing sound. It wasn't the shrub before us or the one behind, but the bush next to us as we walked by. We were not touching them or even near them. It happened all the way to the car.

A Catholic priest, a Hawaiian man from the little church down on Waianae Valley Road, came to bless the property. He is dead now himself. I asked him what he was going to do and explained that we didn't want her harmed. She wasn't an awful person. We just wanted her to be quiet.

He said he was helping her to move onto the next space. But I am also blessing all of you, he continued, because if you should leave the land she might come back.

"Well, that is a blessing," we said, "and besides the landlord likes her." At least we were still able to laugh about it.

After the blessing, we all moved back and it was quiet for a year until we left for good. We had found another place and we were slowly moving out, staying at the new place but returning to collect our stuff and clean up. Although we didn't mention it to each other then, we suddenly felt as though the ghost was back.

We were on good terms with both our landlord and landlady until the day we were to leave when both of them suddenly flipped out. They fell into a rage and became hysterical yelling the craziest things. Our landlady began walking back and forth shouting, "If I had a knife, I would stab all of you. Don't go! I'm going to stab you to stop you. Do you want me to shoot your heads off?"

Our landlady had always been a gentle person and had never done anything like that before. There was no reason for her behavior. All we could do was to get out of there as fast as we could.

Later we compared notes and all agreed that we had felt the presence of the ghost as we were preparing to move out. I don't think she was gone after the place was blessed. I think she was just quiet. I think she will always be there.

The Ghostly Voyeur

Marie Stumph was one of the roommates who experienced the Phantom in the Field. This interview was conducted in Waianae.

After we left the place in Waianae Valley, we moved into a cute little house in Maile. I wasn't there the day that Mark and the others left Hawaii for good. My mother is Peruvian and I had traveled to Peru. I was in Manchu Picchu at the time, but I was having vivid dreams about Mark and Hugh on the day they left our old house. When I came back to the Islands and went home to the Maile house, I found that my roommates had given me the biggest bedroom. I was surprised and thought how nice it was for them to save it for me. No one said a word and I moved into my bedroom. They didn't want to worry me, but shortly after they told me the truth: *Nobody else wanted that room because there was a ghost in there too!* My dear roommates had saved it all for me.

One night, while I was in South America, Mark and Hugh were alone in the new house when they heard a thud coming from my bedroom. Thinking that an intruder had broken in, they crept down the hallway and listened outside of the bedroom door. They clearly heard noises in the room that sounded like someone pacing back and forth and moving things around. Certain that someone had come in through the window to steal things, they went to get their knives and bravely burst into the room. No one was there. The room was totally empty. The curtains were flying in the air, but as soon as they entered the room, both the curtains and noises instantly died down and all was quiet. They closed the door, put their knives away and went back to their own room with a mutual promise not to tell me what had happened that night.

We lived in the house for two years. During that time, doors would open and close by themselves, especially when people were making love. The ghost would make his entrance at the oddest times... I think he was a kind of voyeur! I say "he" as the energy of his presence felt masculine. He was not a bothersome ghost; he was very low key.

My boyfriend Phillip was spending every night with me and he doesn't believe in ghosts. I said, "Fine! Sleep right here." During the night, the door would fly open and then it would close. It would be like, "Okay, we know why you're here. Who's watching?" It was not like the woman's ghost in the valley had been. She was persistent and intense and lonely. She wanted to talk. Our voyeur wasn't a busybody and didn't go crawling into our heads or try to chat us up. He never told anyone a story; we didn't know his history; he wasn't threatening the way she had been. He would just open and close doors and sometimes he would make a lot of noise. It seemed that the door would always open during sex and we would say, "Oh, here he is again!" But he wasn't oppressive or scary when he made his presence known and it didn't really feel like much of an intrusion. He was just there.

Our neighbor, Mrs. Gibson, confirmed our suspicions that the house was haunted. She had lived next door in a tiny cottage for ten years. One day she said to me, "Yeah Marie, you inherited the ghost when you moved in!" My friend Franny, who lived right down the road, also told me that she had heard there was a ghost in our house, so it seemed that his reputation had preceded us.

That was my second ghost... Would you believe there was a third?

After I left the little house in Maile, I moved in with my friend Felicia in Waianae town. She lived in a modern Hicks tract house and she didn't tell me that we had another invisible roomie. Fine with me. I don't want to hear about your little trip! Well, I moved my furniture in and we painted the walls white. Just the two of us were supposed to be living in the house. It wasn't long however that I was awakened with the feeling that someone—not Felicia!—was standing in the doorway looking at me. After three nights of this, I felt as though someone had walked right into the room and was staring down at me. This continued for several nights until one night I awoke feeling as though someone was on top of me holding me down. This happened several times. I would be sound asleep only to be abruptly awakened with the feeling of a heavy weight on top of me. I wasn't able to open my eyes, sit up or call out, but I was able to do my Hawaiian protection chant. Then it would lift and leave.

One morning I awoke to discover that I had fingerprints marking my body in many places like bruises that lasted about three days. I thought uh oh, this is getting serious. Then I discovered a mysterious spot coming through my freshly painted walls and another spot coming up through the floor. It looked like an oil spill only it wasn't oil. It was dark and viscous and thick. I didn't know where it came from or how it got there as it didn't come from the ceiling and we didn't have a pet.

I was teaching school at the time and I had to go to class every day. I began to wear long-sleeved blouses so I wouldn't come to school looking like a battered housewife. I didn't want the students asking questions. My friend and I were teaching together and Franny is Hawaiian, so I felt I could ask her about what was happening. When I told her about the ghost in Felicia's house, she wasn't surprised. In fact, she already knew about it. She had also heard about the inexplicable spots on the ceiling and the rug. She called it "devil shit." She told me of a house in Pattaya, Thailand, that is supposedly haunted by the soul of a Thai girl who had killed herself there in despair when her Belgian lover left her to return to his wife and children. She had cut her wrists and bled to death in the front room. The house could not be rented after that, even to weekend visitors, because a stain was seen coming up through the linoleum carpet on the teakwood floor of the room where she had died. Sobs and moans would rend the night audible to whoever was in the house. If the stain were removed, it would reappear and renew itself. The owner of this haunted house redesigned the room into a very large storage closet and paid a group of ghost chasers to exorcise the place. However, the stain persists and renters will not stay in the house to this day. (*Bangkok Post*, Sunday, May 11, 1986, Donald E. Bott, "Thai Ghosts Show No Lack of Spirit.")

I decided that it was time to talk to Felicia. She was unperturbed when I told her and said, "I know my ghost. I've been in this house for six years."

She went on to tell me that she didn't mind his hanging about the place as she figured that it was his house and land. She felt he was a Hawaiian man and she had been communicating with him for a long time. He didn't frighten her and she didn't want him to go away. When I suggested having the house blessed, she reluctantly agreed but each time I made arrangements with the minister, she would cop out. I didn't want to be pushy as it was her house first. I finally asked her point blank whether she wanted to do it or not. She admitted that she did not because she felt it might chase her ghost away, but then she relented saying, "It's your house too. You have rights. Let's just do it."

We went to a little church on Plantation Row by Ono Street. The person we talked to was Hawaiian and he looked at us as if we didn't belong in Waianae because we were both *haoles* (white people). He gave us "stink eye" and actually told us we were not supposed to be there and the ghost was giving us reason to move. Well, that got our backs up! Felicia and I got out of there and we never did get the house blessed.

I continued to feel the ghost's presence in the bedroom and hall, but I told myself, "No more ghosts! I don't need to share your space and you don't need to share mine!"

Then Kathy moved in.

One morning we were all having breakfast in the kitchen, and Kathy's eyes were looking really tired and she said, "You guys..."

"What, Kathy?"

"You didn't tell me."

We looked at each other.

"Is there a ghost in this house?" she continued.

We started to apologize like crazy. "We're sorry we didn't tell you..."

She went on. "The first night he was standing in the door. The second night it was the same. The third night he crossed the threshold and from then on he started to talk in my head when I tried to sleep!"

And we said, "Yeah, that's basically our experience!"

The Haunted Mansion

Lim Tien Soo Ph.D. was a visiting professor of Botany from Malaysia associated with the East West Center at the University of Hawaii. After spending over twenty years in the United States, he returned to Malaysia where he currently lives.

In the western world we want to prove everything. We want to quantify everything and if we cannot measure a thing, we say it's not there. *But in Asia, spirits are part of every aspect of daily life.* We communicate with them in the same way that you and I are sitting here talking together. Of course, in order to do that you must go through proper mediums or people who know. It's like tuning the radio: if you can't get the right frequency you can't hear the song even though the music is passing by in the airwaves. KDEO is going on right now and we hear nothing because we are not tuning in.

I am a Taoist Buddhist and I don't think you will find a Taoist Buddhist who does not believe in ghosts. Right from the beginning of life, even before the day an infant comes into this world, the spirit realm is playing a part. Parents already know whom the person is and whom to expect, even before the baby is born. My mother had seven daughters. One night she had a dream. In her dream, Kwan Yin, the Goddess of Mercy, came to her to grant her wish for a boy. Kwan Yin spoke to her and said, "You have a garland of red blossoms. I will send you a white blossom. I will choose a soul from Heaven myself. You will have your son." Soon after, I was born.

Not only is communication with the spirit world possible in dreams, there are other non-verbal ways. If you have been to a Taoist Temple, you may have seen the two halves of a seed that are used to receive messages. One side is flat and one side has a hump; now suppose I want to ask a question. "Is my friend coming to my house today?" I don't know the answer, right? So

I hold the two parts of the seed together and ask. Then I throw the thing down. If both sides are flat, the answer is no. If both sides are up, the question is humorous and there is no need for an answer. If one side is down and one side is up, the answer is yes. This is only one way to get answers from the spirit world.

In Asia we believe that spirits are always around us because we exist in the same realm. The good spirits are always following us, guiding us, while the bad spirits are trying to attack us, to misguide us.

I have actually seen ghosts myself. When I was growing up as a rural boy in Malaysia, I lived in a small village in the country, but I worked in a store in the nearby city. Every day after school I would ride my bicycle to work in the city and back through the jungle to my village at night. I was pedaling home through the path of the jungle rather late one night and it was pitch black. I noticed an old grandmother crossing the road. I thought it very late for her to be out. She was bathed in a shining blue light as bright as day. I called out to her, "Amah, may I help you?" But she appeared not to hear me. I called out to her once more and again she appeared not to hear me. Thinking that she was hard of hearing, I alighted from my bicycle and walked towards her but as I approached...*she disappeared*! It was then that I realized that she was of the spirit world. She was a ghost.

There are other experiences. One night I happened to be sleeping in an unlocked car on a city street. I often spent the night in this way when it was too late to go home. I was in the front seat when I saw four tiny figures about six inches tall dance across the dashboard of the car to a kind of polka. I actually heard what sounded like bluegrass fiddle music. They too were shining with the same bright blue light. All they did was dance to the music and then they disappeared. Later I asked the old man at our temple about what I had seen. He told me that the little figures belonged to the fairy world and were of the "little people dimension." He explained that they exist simultaneously with the "rough people" (human beings) and the "fine people" (spirits or ghosts). He went on to say that each is in his own dimension, but that all are people.

One night a buddy was with me. He was sleeping in the back seat of a car and it was his habit to get up in the middle of the night to go to the bathroom. This particular night, he had squatted by the side of a drainage ditch when a "bamboo ghost" suddenly confronted him—two tall skinny legs with no body. It just stood there. Needless to say, my friend gave up his midnight relief!

Another time I was asleep in a car; it was very hot and my two feet were sticking out of the open window. The car was parked by the bank of a river. There was a hut on the edge of the water. I woke up in the middle of the night to adjust the position of my legs. I looked out of the car window and saw the figure of a woman drift through the front door of the hut onto the porch. She was about twelve inches above the floor and she was bathed in the same bright blue light. She smoothly, slowly, and gracefully drifted out over the river and "stood" over the water. As I watched, she turned to look around, slowly sunk into the water, and disappeared.

People in Asia like to sit down and tell ghost stories, but no one there would be frightened. Rather they would look for a proper way of resolving the problem. Perhaps this story will illustrate the difference in perception towards ghosts in the east and in the west.

It was during the Japanese occupation of Malaysia in World War II. Wherever the Japanese would go they would always head for the richest family in the biggest house to establish their headquarters. In my village, there was a huge stone mansion on a hill between my house and my school. Everyday my brothers and sisters and I would have to walk past this house. It was a beautiful place, but it had been used as a Japanese headquarters during the occupation and since that time no one had been able to live there. Many terrible things happened during that era. People had been tortured there and some had even had their heads cut off. Many times vagrants or poor families would try to move into that house, but at night they would be bothered by a terrible commotion as if there were a million people present and of course no one else was there at all and they would be scared out of their wits and leave. So the house had stood vacant all of those years.

Now the Japanese occupation was in the early 1940s and it wasn't until 1970 that a man moved into the house determined to stay. He was totally broke, he had a family to care for, and he was desperate. He declared that he was going to stay in the house whether the ghosts liked it or not and bravely said that he was ready for all that might happen. He was going to put up with whatever came and he was not going to be chased out no matter what. Sure enough, they moved in and the same things occurred. During the day, nothing disturbed them but at night, all night long, there was tremendous activity as if a crowd of people were talking, laughing, crying, taking showers, brushing their teeth, and all of that. The man paid no attention however and he and his family continued to live there.

Finally one night a spirit appeared to him and said:

"I represent all of my friends who are with me. We have no homes to go to. Nobody has ceremoniously guided us into the next world. We are caught here. Will you help us?"

The man replied that he could not help, as he had no money. The spirit pleaded with the man and promised to help him obtain the money if he would only consent to hold a proper ceremony for all of the ghosts who had been bound to the mansion for the last thirty years. The man then agreed to give them a ceremony if only there were money to do so. The spirit then gave him four numbers and instructed him to buy these numbers in the lottery. In doing so the man was guaranteed a winning of $10,000. However he was warned that he must keep his promise; he was not to grab the money and run!

The man bought the numbers that the spirit had given him and sure enough he did win the $10,000. He kept his promise to the ghosts in the mansion and gave them an elaborate ceremony to free their spirits. Henceforth, the mansion was peaceful unto this day.

In Asia the spirit world is symbolically treated just like our world in the belief that ghosts need to live as we do: they need to eat, to work, to drive a car, etc. So people make paper houses, paper cars, paper servants, and everything else they think the spirits might need to be comfortable in heaven. If there are thirty spirits, then thirty of everything is provided. The paper cutouts are then burned during a ceremony in order to send it all into the *other* world. Once this is done, then it may be said that everybody is accounted for, they are all happy, and it's time for them to go on.

During these ceremonies, it's also necessary for the spirits to have someone living in this world to usher them into the next world. For instance, when my grandmother died, I was the one chosen to lead her into the other world. Certain beliefs, such as the belief that spirits are not able to cross water until someone in their ancestral line invites them to cross that water, must be observed. During my grandmother's ceremony I had to kneel before every drain and stream before her coffin could pass that spot on the way to the cemetery. I had to pray with my head on the ground to invite my grandmother to pass through this water. It was for this reason that the ghosts in the mansion were pleading with the man to ceremoniously lead them on into the next world. In Malaysia an unoccupied dwelling may be claimed after years of occupancy and that is how a poor man became the owner of the mansion on the hill.

Plantation Ghost Tales

Nobu Kotano is a social worker in Honolulu. He was the Training Coordinator for the Division of Vocational Rehabilitation of the Department of Social Services and Housing for many years. Of Japanese descent, he grew up on the Big Island of Hawaii.

During World War II, I was a kid growing up on Naalehu Plantation on the Big Island. It was a little plantation about seven miles beyond Pahoa towards South Point. It's still there. There were several hundred people living at Naalehu so it was rather self-contained. There was no hospital, but there was a clinic with one doctor. My sister was the only nurse and being the only nurse, she also had to be the ambulance driver. Being the ambulance driver meant she encountered all kinds of strange things in the middle of the night. Whenever there were patients to take to the hospital in Pahoa, she had to drive the ambulance over narrow cane haul roads. These roads were nothing more than lava rocks near the ocean in some places, a typically Hawaiian kind of thing.

One dark night she was driving her ambulance to Pahoa when she saw lights coming towards her. She took them to be two headlights and automatically slowed down as the road was narrow and she thought another car was approaching. The oncoming lights also slowed down. My sister slowed even more thinking that she would approach the oncoming vehicle very carefully, meet it and negotiate around the bend, but the closer she got to the lights the slower they approached. She didn't think much about it until suddenly the lights went out. She stopped the ambulance and waited thinking that the other driver must have lost his lights. She waited and waited. The car never did approach. When she carefully resumed her travel, there was no car in sight in any direction. There was simply nothing there. She finally stopped

39

and picked a couple of ti leaves by the side of the road to keep in the ambulance for the rest of the trip to Pahoa.

Puna is a heavy area. One incident that came out of that place had to do with a surveyor for the plantation whom I knew fairly well because he had a work shed right in back of our house. He was a Japanese man who used to spread all his blueprints out in his shed. As a kid I was allowed to roam in there and talk to him. He was the only surveyor for the plantation and he would go up in the hills, into the cane fields, and all over the place. There were many old Hawaiian caves there and one day he stumbled upon a cave and found some artifacts. Not knowing any better, he brought them home with him. It wasn't long before he was desperately ill and the doctors could not figure out what was wrong. He went to a specialist and he couldn't discover the cause of his illness either. Finally somebody got wind of the fact that he had broken one of the most sacred of the Hawaiian *kapus* by disturbing a burial cave and he was told that he must return the artifacts. This he was only too happy to do and shortly thereafter he recovered. I remember watching him put the artifacts back in the cave. After that experience he knew very well not to repeat his mistake.

The area around Puna is indeed a mysterious place. My uncle and cousins lived at the Olaa Plantation, nine miles from Hilo. The beach club there used to have a bunch of mansions for their managers and administrators and many of these old places are still there. My uncle was one of the caretakers of this plantation and I remember spending wonderful summers there as a boy. My uncle lived in one of the little row houses provided by the plantation for caretakers. There was a big green lawn and great big trees. The whole area was surrounded with sugar cane so it was a magical place to grow up with. The entire area was reputed to be haunted however—and *HAUNTED* it was.

There was a main road in front of my uncle's place leading to Pahoa and Black Sands Beach (which is now covered with lava). Lining the street was a long row of ironwood trees. Now these trees figure in

Japanese lore quite often, as they are ghostly looking trees with all of those leaves hanging down. This was during the Second World War and a squad of U.S. soldiers was stationed right underneath those trees to monitor the road because it led to the ocean. Those poor soldiers from the mainland would have a hard time with the Hawaiian ghosts! They would see and hear all kinds of things after dark and get all excited and shoot their guns off in the middle of the night.

One of the most frequent phenomena that bothered them were the *sinotama* or **fireballs**. (*Si* is "fire" and *tama* is "ball" in the Japanese language. The phenomenon occurs in Japan too.) These fireballs behave in very strange ways. They appear to be balls of light that fly about through the air very erratically. One night the soldiers opened fire at a bombardment of fireballs and it was really funny. The next morning they went to look for traces of whatever it was that they had been shooting at and they found blood. Upon further investigation, they discovered a dead cow that had wandered off from its pasture into the fray, went into the cane field, and died, a casualty of a midnight spook attack!

My cousin had an experience with *sinotama* however that was really spooky. He was an avid fisherman and liked to go out fishing at night. He was particularly fond of a delicacy called sea cucumber and whenever there was a party he liked to serve it. Often he and his friends would venture out into the ocean late at night in search of sea cucumbers. One night they were knee-high in the water fishing when a bluish-red fireball came at them from out of nowhere. This one didn't fly around the way most of them did. It came close and later he said that it looked like one of those camp lanterns that you pump gas into—a bright blue light with red flecks here and there. They said it was real because you could see its reflection in the water. It hovered by them for a few minutes and then it just swooshed away.

In Japan the *sinotama* is so famous that my mother used to tell us stories that she had heard when she was growing up. These stories defined the fireball as the soul or essence of a dying person, a kind of physiological life force that leaves the body at death and catches fire. These *sinotama* not only come from people, but from animals and birds as well. My mother told us one lovely story that she remembered of an old couple that lived near her when she was a little girl. After a long lifetime spent together, the old woman finally died one day and was buried. A couple of weeks later, the husband took sick and followed his wife to the grave. On the night that he died, the neighbors all witnessed an incredible phenomenon. Before their amazed eyes, they saw a fireball emerge from the old woman's grave just as another flew from the house of her dying husband. The fireballs encircled each other and then flew away together. Romantic nonsense, no? And that was my mother telling me that story! So in Japan, *sinotama* are well known.

The Blue Lights of Saddle Road

Ah Fat Lee is retired from the Hawaii State Parks Department. He was instrumental in implementing the successful program to save the Hawaiian Nene birds from extinction. He and his wife Barbara live on the Big Island, where they shared their separate experiences with the infamous Blue Lights of Saddle Road.

I used to work for the Hawaii State Parks Department up on Saddle Road. There was a cabin located on Mauna Kea that the hunters used. It was originally built for the forest rangers who worked around the mountains some fifty years ago. Transportation was difficult then. There were no roads up there and the fences had to be checked on foot or on horseback. When night fell, you stayed in the cabin. It was only in later years that it became a hunters' cabin.

I've slept in that cabin many times. Strange things happened at night to some people but not to others, yet the stories persist. I have heard quite a few of the hunters tell about doors that open and slam shut for no reason at all when there is no breeze. Some have heard Hawaiian music when there is no one there. I remember one *haole* (Caucasian) guy with one leg who loved to go out and stay in the cabin. He couldn't climb hills, but he sure liked to go out and stay in the cabin. One afternoon he had stayed behind after the hunters had gone after their game. He heard the Hawaiian music very clearly and he told everybody about it when they got back.

One night we had all been walking around the mountains doing fieldwork and we were really tired when we got back to the cabin. The cook was a Portuguese guy and he was really old. He slept near the old wood stove and that night he got "choked"—woke up yelling his head off and woke up all the rest of us as well. Nobody appreciated that much!

I was accustomed to hearing all kinds of stories about Saddle Road and that area of the Big Island, so when I came across the blue lights myself I wasn't totally unprepared.

It must have been in the 1960s when I first SAW it: *a small bright blue light that floats around and stays up in the air*. It doesn't bother anybody. I've seen it maybe fifteen or twenty times over the years, maybe more. I never counted. Hawaiians believe that it's an *akualele,* a spirit. I know that when I stopped the car I was driving at the time, the light stopped too and hovered in the air. When I started the car and drove away, the light began to follow me again.

It seems that there was a prison camp in the area at one time. There is a big *akualele*—a very old one—that many people associate with that place. I was living up there in the 1930s, working for the land. I had seen that particular light many times off the highway by the road. There's a favorite story that people used to tell about it that goes like this:

It was in the days of the old one-room schoolhouse and there was a teacher who had a quarry. One day he wanted to go to Waimea. Now in the old days, there were a lot of cattle drives and gates to control the cattle that were all over. Nowadays there are fences along most highways so the cattle won't get on the road, but back then they had gates. The school teacher offered to take one of his students, a young Hawaiian boy, to Waimea with him if he would help him to open and close the gates so he wouldn't have to keep jumping in and out of the car. The boy agreed and they started driving to the town. It was after dark when they reached the particular spot in the road where they saw the light coming towards them. At first, the teacher thought it was a car approaching them as it was headed straight for their own vehicle. Thinking they might crash, he tried to avoid it and drove his own car right off the road. Both the teacher and the boy were unhurt, but the car was stuck fast in a ditch. They couldn't get it back onto the road, so they started to walk through the woods to Waimea. It was at least a five-mile walk and it was pitch black. The light followed the schoolteacher and the boy all the way! It would swoop back and forth over their heads. When it would come close, the man would say to the boy, "Come on Sam, lay down and let's hide!" Down they would go and the light would fly off. As soon as they would start to walk again, the thing would come back and start hovering around them. They finally got to Waimea at 1 o'clock in the morning, shaken but unhurt.

The weird follow-up to the story happened the next day. A bunch of guys were driving from Waimea to Waikii when one of them said, "Pull over quick! I just saw the school teacher's car." They pulled over at the junction of Saddle and Kona Roads and got out to investigate. There was the teacher's car sitting on top of the cattle gate!

My wife, Barbara, has also seen the blue lights...

Barbara's Story

Yes, I have had an experience with the blue lights of Saddle Road myself. This was about five years ago. We were living in Pohakaloa and I was driving down to Waimea to go to a meeting. It was very late when I returned home. I was right at the junction and there was a light bobbing out in the open area there. I didn't see it at first, but the car ahead of me must have because all of a sudden he turned around and went scooting back for Waimea at a tremendous clip.

I turned up Saddle Road and it was then that I noticed this light following me. It was very bright and it went on the other side of the *puu*, the cinder pit, and then flew over to the *kona* side of the pit, came out, and followed me up to the pine trees as far as Waikii.

I slowed down to get a better look at it and I almost drove right off the road. It was just beyond the telephone lines and there was no logical reason for a light to be there. There is no habitation and it was too high up in the air to be someone on a horse. It's all pasture and fenced-in paddock land and the light was skipping over fences without a break.

I slowed the car and finally stopped. The light *slowed and stopped* too. I didn't get out, but I leaned across the passenger side and peeked out the window at it. The light hovered in the air for several minutes. Then it left with a *swoosh* and was gone.

I wasn't very frightened. I'm made of the same stuff as my husband, Ah Fat. He has generations of Chinese heritage in back of him to allay his fear. I'm not Chinese, but I've got education and curiosity and that allays fear I think. It did flash through my mind that maybe the light was a UFO or an entity—a viable entity—that you could converse with, but with all of my training, education, and beliefs, I had to have hard facts and data before I could accept these possibilities. The possibility of little green men from God knows where crossed my mind about as long as the possibility of marsh gas did. If I were to analyze the steps of my thinking process at that moment,

I was reviewing all the possibilities I could come up with, and I still didn't have a probability. It's an unknown, but it happened. It has happened before and it will probably happen again.

The Sitting Ghost of Maunakea

This interview with Barbara Lee took place on the Big Island on August 22, 1984.

There are more things in the universe than I have dreamt of and some things are unknown. What happened to me that night is unknown and yet, IT happened.

I was staying at the Mauna Kea Beach Hotel. I had checked in early that evening after having flown straight in from the Mainland. Although I'd stayed at the hotel quite a few times before, this was the first time I had been in the newer beach wing. I went to dinner and did all of the usual puttery (trifling) things people do before retiring for bed.

I woke up at 3:30 in the morning. It was dark and I couldn't see a thing. I was sleeping on my tummy and there was *something* on my back pressing me to the bed. I looked both ways, but I couldn't move and I couldn't turn over. I still get "chicken skin" just thinking about it! I really can't remember if I got an arm loose first or if I just rolled off the bed. I immediately turned the lights on and there wasn't anything in the room except me. I went to the phone and called the front desk. I told them that I wanted out of that room immediately and within ten minutes I was out with all of my things. The next thing I knew, I was ensconced in a room in the main building that I had been in before.

I thought about what had happened. I wasn't drunk and I wasn't crazy. There were no physiological or psychological reasons for a thing like that to happen. *IT* just did.

There wasn't anybody on the hotel staff who didn't believe me. Here it was after 3 o'clock in the morning and they were all more than happy to help me switch rooms. Later one of the maids came to talk to me in private. She told me confidentially that the whole new section of the beach wing had been built over a *heiau* and a gravesite and that it hadn't been properly blessed. She said that the same phenomena had happened to others who had stayed in that room. She thought that I had the worst experience of any *haole* in that section.

The hotel had been built in 1960. It must have been sometime in the early 1970s when the new wing was built on the kona side. She told me that the hotel had been blessed several times, but that it must have been too late because it did not seem to be effective.

I'm not a fearful person, but it took me many years before I was able to talk about that experience to a good friend, let alone an acquaintance. I know I won't ever willingly go back and stay in that section of the hotel again. Ever!

There are ghostly occurrences at every hotel along the Kona coast. The King's Highway runs along there, you know, and there's a marvelous story about a Hawaiian warrior who appears at the Sheraton hotel. He is a very big tall broad Hawaiian who wears a *mahiole* (headdress) and a feather cloak and who carries a spear. Sometimes he appears on the roof and sometimes he mingles with the guests. The hotel had a terrible time keeping personnel for a while before word got around that he was very gentle and meant no harm. Usually only Hawaiian people see him, but *haole* guests have seen him too. Luckily most of them assume that he has been hired by the hotel to supply local atmosphere!

The Pig Hunt

Charlie Lee is Ah Fat Lee's cousin and a native of the Big Island.

You can make fun of these "pork over the Pali" stories all you want, but these things actually happen. It happened to me. Most of my life was spent working off of the island for the engineering firm Morris and Knutsen on a civilian contractual basis all over the world. I have traveled from Vietnam to Zaire, but I love to hunt so I used to time my visits home to Hawaii in order to be here during the hunting season.

Once many years ago, I went hunting on the Big Island with my cousin, Ah Fat, and several men from Honolulu. We had gone after pigs in the mountains where Saddle Road is today. We were on the trail to Kona, a trail that was well used because there was no road there at the time. In ancient times Hawaiian warriors used the trail. Today the Nalani Hotel stands on that location. We liked to use that trail when we went hunting because it was paved with *'ili'ili*, flat rocks, used by the ancient Hawaiians in hula to make music and provide a beat for the dance. The rocks glittered in the moonlight and made the trail easy to follow at night. On this particular trip we were camped in a cabin on the trail by a big fishpond. The pond survives to this day and is located on the Nalani Hotel grounds.

We had had a successful trip of it that day. There were a lot of wild hogs in the *keawe* bushes and we had each gotten our meat down to the last man. We had the animals slung over our shoulders, which we had padded with *ti* leaves so that the weight of the pigs wouldn't dig into our backs. Of course, according to Hawaiian tradition this was a good luck thing to do too in order to appease any spirits that might be lurking in the night. We had all done this except for the old man of our group, Willie Macau. By the time he got to the *ti* leaves there weren't any left so he just slung the pig over his shoulder and came down the hill behind me.

Daylight was fading and we realized that we couldn't get back to camp before dark. I was in the lead carrying the rifle, Willie was next, and Ah Fat and the rest were following along behind. We had a big hunting dog following Willie.

Soon it was pitch dark. I joked with the guys and told them that maybe *ti* leaves were not enough protection against those spirits out there that just love pork. I even suggested that they cut off little pieces of meat and drop them as they walked so that they wouldn't lose their pigs. They all laughed at that, but I was half serious.

Although I'm pure Chinese, I always felt that it was a good idea to honor Hawaiian traditions, so I got out my pocketknife and cut off little pieces of my pork to leave as offerings along the trail. I had no idea whom I was appeasing, maybe Kamapuaa, the pig god. The trail we were hiking was more or less a dividing line. According to legend, Pele, the volcano goddess, has Moana Loa on the south end of the island, Kamapuao has Mauna Kea on the north end, and Saddle Road seemed to be the dividing line between the two mountains.

Although the night was dark the *'ili'ili* sparkled in the moonlight and made the trail relatively clear to follow. We were hiking along at a good clip in spite of the burdens on our backs when suddenly some of the guys veered off the trail and went crashing down into the brush.

"Come back to the trail!" I cried. "My God, follow the trail!"

But they continued to thrash around in the *keawe* and yelled back that they were on the trail and that I was the one who was not. It was the weirdest thing…these guys crashing through the brush going in all directions with no trail under them and yet they thought they saw a trail! They continued in this vein for several minutes until I finally heard them shouting, "Hey, what's going on? Where's the trail?" I wondered myself what was going on. Our dog had stayed on the trail with me and was cowering and whimpering with all of his hair standing straight up on end. He was a good dog and had never behaved that way before.

Finally Macau and the rest came thrashing back to the trail with great commotion. They seemed to be okay and appeared unhurt except for one thing: no pigs on their backs! When I asked what had happened to their meat they all agreed that it had just been lifted off their backs. At first I thought they were putting me on and having a good practical joke of it, but after looking at their expressions, I realized they were telling the truth.

"Eh, come on!" I said. "Eight-pound hogs don't just disappear into thin air. We go look. You guys must have dropped them in the *keawe*. Let's go see."

We went back to where all the yelling had been to search for the meat. There was nothing. Not a sign of pork in the vicinity anywhere. But how are you going to find anything in the dark? We decided to camp and come back in the morning. Nights are cold in the mountains so the meat would be fresh.

We made our way back to camp without the meat. Our dog slunk back with his tail between his legs and kept whimpering until we were inside the cabin. We tried to make heads or tails of what had happened, but each guy told the same story. He thought he was on the trail until he felt his pig being lifted off his back into the air. Then he realized he was deep in the brush and became wildly confused. Everyone agreed on what they had experienced.

We were all exhausted and tried to turn in. Poor Macau didn't sleep all night. He kept hearing footsteps on the trail outside. The *haole* guy with him heard them too, but when we checked there was nothing there. Old Willie accused us of fooling with him, but we had done nothing. The old Hawaiian trail ran right by the front of our cabin, but no one passed there during the night.

The next morning after the sun had finally risen, we returned to the spot where the meat had disappeared. We spent over an hour searching every inch of the terrain in all directions, tracing then retracing our tracks of the night before. We could not find a trace of the pigs, not anywhere! It is a mystery to this day. Only the pig I carried on my back survived the trek on that ancient trail. But then I was the only one of the party to offer my bits of pork to the spirits. I wonder…

The White Lady of Ka'anapali

Clarence Sakai was employed as security guard for a major hotel in Ka'anapali, Maui, when this interview was taken. He asked that his real name be withheld out of concern for his position.

They call her "White Lady." She has been seen up and down the Ka'anapali strip by approximately a thousand people in the last few years, *kamaaina (old timer)* and *malihini* (newcomer) alike.

Although she roams around and appears whenever and wherever she pleases, she has made it a tradition to appear annually in the banquet kitchen of our hotel on the night of June 17. She has appeared there for the past five years at 3 a.m. Most of the workers who have seen her were immigrants of Vietnamese or Filipino extractions and they all quit their jobs and did not return. One guy was cleaning the kitchen when she appeared. He didn't speak English fluently, but he tried to tell her that the kitchen was off limits to guests. She turned away at the sound of his voice and it was then that he noticed that the lady didn't have legs! She was floating several feet off of the ground. He told his supervisor and then just walked out. A year later—on the same date and about the same time—another cleaning person saw the same sight: *White Lady, no legs*. He ran out the door and didn't even bother to quit!

One night as I was getting off work, two guys from the hotel came running into the loading dock and, I swear, they were hysterical. They were freaking out. I asked them what was going on and they kept yelling, "White Lady! I'm not going back in! I'm not going in!" They said they had seen her wearing what looked like a wedding dress and that she floats a few feet off of the ground. She just stands with her arms outstretched and her palms upwards. Then she turns and floats away.

I *saw* her four years ago in the front lobby. I was a Security Guardsman for two years and I was on duty that night. It was about 2 a.m. I caught her in a glance from the corner of my eye at first so I didn't think much about it. When I looked up, she was standing beside the large blue and white Chinese vase by the front entrance. She was about twenty or thirty feet away from me by the mirror on the right hand side of the doors. She was dressed all in white lace and there were ruffles on her sleeves. It looked like a wedding dress.

She was *haole* and had long dark hair hanging to the middle of her back. She was standing with both arms outstretched and her palms facing upwards as if to say, "Where is he?" I thought she was a hotel guest and I said, "Pardon me, Mum, but it doesn't look good if you walk around in your nightgown. You shouldn't really be out alone at this time of night." At the sound of my voice, she started to turn away. It was then that I realized that not only was her gown transparent, but the rest of her was too! I could see right through her! She glided smoothly around the corner and I ran after her. It couldn't have taken me more than two or three seconds to reach the spot she had been in, but there was nobody there. She had vanished. She was gone.

So many people have seen her, both hotel workers and guests. There is a story that explains why she keeps appearing. She was going to be married on June 17, they say, and she was killed the day before her wedding.

Many strange things have happened in this hotel since I have worked here. It was built over an old burial site and a cemetery and you can still see the remains of the old graveyard at the end of the strip next to our hotel. It seems that most of the gravesites are located under the Atrium Tower, which is where most of the stuff happens. That tower is heavy! There is a room under the tower with a steel door that's got a wheel on it like a submarine and a little window covered with chicken wire. There is an alarm on it that is activated by the crack of a seal. The security guards showed me the place and said that when they built the hotel, they cleared all of the graves and put the bones from the construction site in that place. Some of the hotels had the grounds blessed and some didn't. I'm guessing that this one didn't!

There are two rooms on the first floor of the Atrium Tower that are really spooky. Guests who stay there complain of strange noises at night and other things. Now the tower starts on the fourteenth floor and is hollow underneath so it is sixty feet above the front desk of empty space. One night we received a call from the people in Room

1401 complaining that someone was hammering beneath their floor with something solid and the noise was disturbing them. I went up with another security guard to investigate. We walked into the room and we could hear sawing and hammering noises pounding away underneath the floor. It was a real racket and yet we *knew* that there was nothing underneath the floor but empty space. The only thing we could do was report it to our supervisor and his reaction was, "Well, you can't write a report like that! Who's going to believe you?"

However they do keep records of these instances in the hotel. They have a whole pile of reports hidden somewhere. A lot of people know about it, but of course they don't want it to get out, as it would be bad for business. The supervisors do believe you when you report an experience like that because they have heard so many similar reports.

I have had so many experiences since working for this hotel. One night I was walking my rounds on the first floor again. There was no wind and it was very still. I went by Room 112 and noticed that the door was open and left ajar. I knocked and no one answered. I knocked again and got no response so I called the front desk. Nobody was registered to that room. I decided to investigate and started to push the door open, but just before I touched it, the door swung halfway open on its own. I said, "Hello? Anybody there?" and shone my flashlight into the room. There was no one in back of the door. I stepped back out in the hallway and the door shut halfway by itself. Then it opened. Then it shut back to halfway again. It opened one more time and then it slammed itself shut on me! I said, "Uh oh, time to leave!" and I did.

Another time my partner and I saw a kid run into Room 123 and shut the door. We called in for help and posted a guy outside and a guy in front. The room was totally sealed off and locked from the inside. There was no way for the kid to get out. We called the assistant manager to unlock the door, but when he did, there was nobody in the room!

There's a lot of weird activity in Room 123. Guests who stay there are continually complaining. About three months ago, the bellboy brought in glasses of water at the guest's request. When they went to collect the glasses, they found the cups completely shaved off with just the stands remaining. There was glass all over the room. Some of the goblets had been cut perfectly in half with one half down and the other half still sitting there. Who's going to cut a glass in half and then put it back?

Sometimes Room 123 will be in perfect readiness for guests and when the door is unlocked to admit them, sheets will be shredded, mirrors will be smashed, and the room will be a total wreck though no one has been inside during the interim.

The management staff refuses to shut down these two rooms. They insist that it's a coincidence that people seem to abuse these two rooms all the time when it isn't the guests who are doing the damage at all. Many times, guests will ask questions like "Was anyone singing last night in Room 123?" or "Was anybody screaming last night in Room 123?" It has happened countless times to people who stay in this one part of the hotel.

I have talked to some of the construction workers who worked on the hotel when it was being built. Seems they had quite a few problems putting up this one tower...*the same tower where all of the activity seems to happen*. One of the rooms on the *makai* side had all of its windows blown out—but they were blown into the room and not out of the room. The doors were locked and there was no one inside. Several of the rooms that had been sealed up tight had bloodstains. No one had been inside and the doors were still locked.

The rest of the hotel is not exempt from weird stuff either. There is a walkway in the lobby where the gardens begin. It's the last walkway leading into the garden and it has four steps leading down. As soon as you walk down three steps and hit that third step, you are assaulted by a terrible odor. Have you ever smelled really bad, rotten meat, even worse than a dead dog or cat? I took my supervisor there to experience it too. Sure enough, he smelled it and said, "My God, it smells like somebody died!" We continued to walk down the path and the odor evaporated. It simply disappears. When we went back to the third step, the odor was gone. Three days later, we went to check it out again. We went to the third step and *bang!* There it was again like somebody threw it in your face with a spray. We continued down the path, turned around, and came back and...IT was gone again. There was no wind, no breeze at all, and yet the odor was gone.

Those Napili Gardens are spooky anyway. You know what a lovely, strong scent plumeria blossoms have when they are blooming? Well, there are plumeria trees all over the garden (they are called cemetery trees, by the way) and when you walk through...it smells totally dead, no fragrance at all. If you pick a blossom, it just doesn't smell. There is a gardenia plant there that never blossomed and one day it got a bud—just one—a green and white big old bud. Three months later, the bud was still there in exactly the same shape. It hadn't changed or grown a bit.

A friend of mine is into this *kahuna* stuff. He walked into the garden one night and immediately said, "This is a bad place. This place is *bad!*" He walked up to the gardenia bush with the one bud and the flower bloomed right in front of my eyes! Talk about weird!

There are some heavy stories in all the hotels up and down the Ka'anapali strip. Superstition-wise, some people believe and some don't. Unless an experience happened to you personally, you probably are not going to believe it. If it does happen to you and you finally see it for yourself... well, that's a different matter!

Ulum Bala: Feast of the Hungry Ghosts

Festival of the Hungry Ghosts is a ceremony that originated in India and is now celebrated annually on the fifteenth day of the seventh lunar month throughout all of Asia.

Dr. Glenn Lum is a Buddhist priest serving in Honolulu. He has performed many exorcisms to banish bothersome spirits and says, "Most people just want to get rid of the things!" This interview was conducted at a Chinese Folk Temple in Liliha, Honolulu, on January 28, 1984.

The Feast of the Hungry Ghosts is a wonderful story! It seems that the Lord Buddha had a disciple whose name was Mulian. Evidently Mulian had psychic powers as he could see and hear things denied to others. He had left his home life to become a monk. One day he saw his long-dead mother in purgatory. She had been sent there for eating meat and slaughtering dogs. She was in the form of a *purta*, a hungry ghost. She seemed to be starving. His first reaction was to feed his mother so he picked up his begging bowl and gave it to her. His mother picked up the food in the bowl, but it immediately turned to fire and burned her. The monk was very distressed by this and he gave her water. However, the water also turned to fire and burned her. The mother wept. Why should she not receive the food and drink that her son had offered her?

Mulian went to the Buddha, the historical Buddha. Now the Buddha could read past lives and he saw that the monk's mother had committed many sins and had reincarnated herself as a hungry ghost to atone for her past. Mulian was anguished and asked the Lord Buddha what could be done to help his mother? He was told to gather all of the monks together and to prepare a feast for the wandering souls on the fifteenth day of the seventh moon, the time when the souls from hell are released. All of the food that the monks had begged for on that day was to be placed on a big pyre, burned, and offered to the spirits through prayer. And that is how the Festival of the Hungry Ghosts began.

According to Buddhism, a person becomes a *linghwen* or an immortal soul when he dies. He goes to hell where he is punished for his earthly transgressions and is then reincarnated to try again. If he has no descendants or if his descendants fail to provide for him, he lives in the afterworld as a miserable *goei* or ghost. These *goei* are also called the good brethren, hungry ghosts, or lonely spirits. Therefore there are different kinds of hungry ghosts. Depending on the kind of ghost, the throat passage is often as thin as a needle thereby causing eternal hunger. Even if the food did not turn to fire, it could not go down their throats. By chanting sutras during the ceremony, the throats of the ghosts would be opened for a short time allowing the food to go down. The festival then is a time to feed the spirits, to give them food and drink, to chant for them, to give them clothes and money (this is Chinese now), and to offer them a chance to seek salvation. If they are tired of suffering for aeons, the ceremony offers them a second chance to gain Nirvana. If their sins are deep, they may need many chances. These spirits may have to work on their karma for millenniums, so in Buddhism and in the Chinese religion, we cover all the areas. Since we don't know for sure if one ceremony will do it for the spirits, we repeat it every year. There may be new hungry ghosts or hungry ghosts caught after many lifetimes in that realm of existence still trying to get free.

It is the Buddhist belief that as the spirit passes away from the body on this physical plane, its karma decides where and whom it will reincarnate as perhaps an animal or a human being, perhaps in a limbo state, neither death nor birth, but a wandering on earth. There are many levels of heaven and there are many levels of hell. It's my humble opinion that these levels represent the many levels of human consciousness with the lower levels of consciousness a suffering unto itself. That is hell. Believing this, we symbolically offer these foods. The living never eats the food that is offered on the ground to the homeless ones. It is a Chinese belief that any material object, be it food or whatever, can be infested with either positive or negative energies. If the offered food is eaten, a ghost might go into you and cause you to sicken or otherwise cause havoc with your life. So the cheapest food is prepared and then thrown away. It is the essence that the spirits take because they cannot really eat of course; they just smell.

Ulum Bala is very important as a time to remember ancestors and also as an excuse for the family to get together for lunch or dinner. It is in April and you will hear fireworks in all of the Asian cemeteries, even the newer ones. The fireworks will begin and sacrifices will be made to the family that has gone on before. It is a happy time. In Japan, it is celebrated as *Obon* and is a joyous time. The Japanese have a lighter side and that is why they dance. They say that it is a time for ancestors to come home to visit, to provide them with food, and to be joyful. For the Chinese, it's a time to offer a chance for the spirits to leave their painful existence and to gain salvation with the hope that others may be helped along the way. It's a time to remember your mother, especially because of Mulian's mother.

Sometimes all it takes to release the *goei* is for someone living to tell them to go on. Here in the Hawaiian Islands with all of the ethnic groups we have, often all that is needed is for somebody to tell the spirit to "go away, go someplace else, and don't bother me." It is an especially Chinese approach to say, "I'll provide you with beer and pork and I'll burn money for you, but please go bother somebody else!" If the person is a little more pious, they might say, "Well, I don't want you to go bother somebody else so I will call in a priest and give you a service and then I hope you will eject your consciousness up into Heaven!" Not too many people do that however. Most people call me and say, "Just get rid of IT!" I am called upon many times these days to perform exorcisms.

Some hauntings are attached to specific locations. In some cases, biorhythms may play a part. The Chinese say *luk* cycle, but

I prefer biorhythms as it's a little more scientific. When our bodily rhythms are low, the Chinese believe you can pick up negative energies and bring them home with you. I was told many times by my grandmother not to go swimming during the Hungry Ghost Festival because the gates of hell are open. A restless spirit might want a human body and pull you under the water so they won't have to suffer anymore. If they take over your body, your soul becomes homeless, so we were warned not to go into the water or into the mountains during this time. We were also to be very careful crossing the street. (I went to the beach and the mountains anyway.)

It's important to know how to cleanse and protect yourself from negative spirits. There are many ways. My Hawaiian sources tell me to go to the beach every day to cleanse myself in the salt water of the ocean and this I do. My Christian sources say to protect myself with white light, as do the Buddhists. I have been told to sit on the ground to absorb the tremendous healing energies of the earth or to grab a tree. (Today they say "tree huggers.") There are many things you can do. In all cultures that celebrate the Feast of the Hungry Ghosts, there is a sense of deep love and concern, a caring for all those who have gone before us.

The Demons in the Field

As I child growing up I remember that my grandparents would prepare food on the altar for their ancestors for the afternoon of that day, "Feast of the Hungry Ghosts." From noon until midnight the *prittas*, the ghosts, would come out. That is their time. I saw these spirits, but nobody believes a child so in order not to be reprimanded for "imagining" these things, I learned to keep them to myself. Then as a pre-adolescent, I could hear things. I thought my ears were going bad until much later when I took my training for the ministry in San Francisco, California. I met a beautiful lady, Muriel Olstrom, a Christian minister. One day we were walking in a forest in Marin County. I don't know what made me say it, but I remarked, "Muriel, can you hear that?"

"Yes," she said.

I was so surprised that I had to stop and turn around. "Do you really hear what I am hearing?" I asked.

"Yes," she repeated. "It's a buzzing sound."

Then she assured me that the ringing in my ears was not a sign that my hearing was going bad. She motioned to a large rock and said she perceived an Indian spirit sitting there. She went on to explain the phenomena. From that time on, more of my inner abilities emerged. Many teachers entered my life. Not only a Buddhist master, but Christian ministers, a Sufi, and many more elevated souls taught me universal consciousness.

I had not planned to come home to Hawaii although my doing so was foretold to me during a séance I had attended. I said, "Nah, that's not going to happen! I'm going to stay in California and continue to teach high school." However, I did end up back here. I was also told that my life would eventually revolve around ministering a temple and indeed it has done so. As a teenager, I used to hang around this little folk temple on Liliha Street, where we are right now. I would sit here for hours listening to the old people talk. It has all been collected in my memory bank.

I attended the University of Hawaii and became a teacher. I taught in public schools in San Francisco for five years and during that time I took my final vows as a Buddhist priest. Upon my return to the Islands, I had no church, no following, nothing. I worked out of my apartment and people started to come. The numbers grew through word of mouth as the years went by and I had to move, as my place was too small. Eventually I found myself working at the temple I had attended as a teenage boy.

My most powerful experience with ghosts occurred when I was called to a local high school here in Honolulu (which I cannot name) to exorcise the grounds. It seemed that the students and faculty were being bothered by ghosts—demons actually—springing up from the ground or jumping out from hall lockers as they walked across campus to class. These ghosts were actually seen by the pupils and staff who described them as "human-like." It appeared, upon further investigation, that this phenomenon had taken place generation after generation at this particular school so I was asked, along with other priests of different religions, to rid the school of these spirits… if we could.

Research had shown that the land upon which the school was located had been a Hawaiian battle site long ago. Although priests and ministers had been called in to exorcise the place before, the happenings still occurred. When I walked past the places that were shown to me as spots where demons were known to pop out, I experienced a chamber-like sensation of violent sound energy. It seemed that these ghosts emitted some kind of sound vibration and it was by these energies that I was able to determine whether they were benevolent spirits or mischievous evil ghosts. These demons were definitely evil.

At that time in my life, I was not afraid of anything. I would just say to myself, "Uh oh, here **IT** comes," when the sound began. Then I would go through it in a matter of seconds. *It* felt as though somebody had grabbed the top of my head and pulled something off. *It* was almost as if they were pulling off the energy that was trying to cover me, like a blanket being pulled away. I had never experienced this sensation before and I thought it quite interesting. I even walked backwards to see if it would happen again and it did! Once more I felt the energy cover me and I had the sensation that the demon wanted to suffocate me. I felt *IT* coming all around.

I was sprinkling holy water on the ground and apparently the demon didn't want that and was trying to stop me. The feeling was overwhelming, but even then I was not afraid. I calmly said to myself, "Here *it* comes," and continued to sprinkle the holy water. I remembered what my master had taught me: *When dealing with evil, stay calm and poised and you will overcome.*

"Evil wants you to become agitated and emotionally terrified for that is what it needs to win you, but if you stay calm, poised and have faith in whatever light of consciousness you subscribe to then you will overcome evil."

I also believe that my agency, Lady Kwan Yin, had come to my aid and was pulling off the spirit that was trying to overwhelm me.

The demons that infested this school were some of the people who had died in battle on that site and also some of the evil forces that live in the earth. Many times these evil forces will cause ordinary people to act violently—Lucifer's angels if you like—to prod people into killing each other off. Perhaps these spirits were gutsy to authority and not particularly religious in human life, which would make them hard to get rid of no matter what you did. The consciousness of these souls, the human mind, is so strong that sometimes it just won't leave. The school had been exorcised many times by Christian, Buddhist, and Hawaiian priests; most of the spirits left when it was blessed by a particular Hawaiian priest. He said that many of those spirits had died in battle and he "reincarnated" them by using eggs as a symbol. Each egg symbolized a Hawaiian regiment of twelve warriors. When he threw the eggs into the fire they popped. He explained that with each popping of an egg, the spirits of twelve warriors were released.

Many times when people die, they don't understand that they are dead and think they are still alive. They hang around for generations until one day somebody tells them, "Hey, you're dead! You can go!" Then they leave. It could be these kinds of ghosts who react with consciousness and interact with the living as in the demon who tried to stop my sprinkling of the holy water on the field. Or it could be like an image on a film or tape that simply replays over and over again sans consciousness. Or it could be *kolohe* as the Hawaiians say, just mischievous spirits or poltergeist. It might even be a genuine outreach to say, "I need help! I don't want to stay in this on-going state. I just want to sleep and rest. I want salvation!"

I am still not afraid of these things, but I do realize now that there are dangers involved. Perhaps one day there will be a stronger entity that I cannot take care of by myself. In that case it would take many people with their combined energy to do the job. While I do recognize the dangers, I have full faith in what I believe: *the enlightened beings of the past, present, and future who are always there to protect us.*

The Nature Spirits of Waiahole Valley

Susan Indich was married to Martin Charlot at the time of this occurrence and was the daughter-in-law of famed international artist Jean Charlot, who painted with Diego Rivera in Mexico. Susan was deeply attuned to nature, the Hawaiian Islands, and pohaku (Hawaiian stones). She has five children.

I had moved with my husband and children to the very last house in back of Waiahole Valley. It was located on a little hill in the center of the valley and it was beautiful back there. I found some micro stones so it had been an occupied place from ancient times. I had a very strong feeling about that place. I felt a presence, an *aliveness* there. It wasn't heavy or negative, but the nature spirits were there and I was coming in with my family. I had five children and we were way out in the country. I worried about my kids so after we had lived there for a few months, I decided to go to the mountains to introduce myself and ask permission of the spirits of the place to live in harmony. I always try to make an offering to the spirit of each place where I live, even if it's only a cigarette. Why get off on the wrong track? So I fried some chicken and went to the mountains.

It was sunset when I got there and I suddenly realized that I was about to spend the night by myself. I decided to do everything instinctively so I stood up and faced the mountain and said, "I would like to live in harmony in this place. If this is possible, would you send me a sign?"

And out of nowhere, the thought came into my head to say, "Send me a large bird as a sign that I am accepted."

Then I sat down and made an offering of some chicken to the mountain and the bones to the sea. Why, I don't know. It just seemed the thing to do. Then I waited.

The sky changed color and a flock of birds flew by. I thought, "Ah, birds!" but they were too little and there were too many of them.

The clouds changed color and began to pass over the mountain.

"That's it. The clouds are going to assume the shape of a bird and that will be my sign." I thought, but then said, "Nah, that's not it. Wouldn't it be awful if I didn't get a sign at all? I'm not going to spend the night up here if I'm not wanted. I'm going home!"

Just then from out of the mountain flew a huge Hawaiian owl. It was a whopper! It flew right towards me, circled my head three times and then flew into the valley and out of sight.

"Wow!" I thought. "That was beautiful. I think I'm going to spend the night up here after all."

All of a sudden the owl flew back and this time it was much lower. Again it circled my head three times and flew up to the mountain.

"Hey," I thought, "this is a strong message I'm getting and this is sufficient."

Sure enough, the owl appeared for a third pass. Three times three. It was so low that although I was sitting down, I could feel the wind from its wings. It had a tremendous wingspan and when it flew over my head I thought of my eyes and became frightened. I picked up my slipper and shooed it away.

By then I was awfully excited and I didn't sleep all night. I wanted to see what would happen next and of course nothing did happen except mosquitoes.

The next morning I raced home and called an old Hawaiian friend of the family. Some say she was a *kahuna* (Hawaiian priest). She was a very wise woman. I told her what had happened and that I had shooed it away the third time. I said I wish I hadn't shooed it away.

"Next time," she said, "you will know what to do."

It was a beautiful experience, but I did have mixed feelings. I was thrilled because the message had come through loud and clear. I was also overwhelmed because it was more than I had bargained for. People ask for things and they often get what they ask for. After that I lived in perfect confidence. I was accepted. I never worried about the kids and we never had an accident or a dangerous experience all of the years we lived there. I felt a part of the place and I loved it. I still do.

The Haunted Barge

Tom Rettigan was an executive with a large insurance firm in Honolulu. He shared this experience over lunch at a restaurant in downtown Honolulu. After leaving him, I discovered that the tape in my tape recorder, which had been working perfectly, was completely blank. I immediately sat down on a bench in the mall outside of the restaurant and copied his words from memory.

This happened nine years ago when I was working for Dillingham. We used to tow heavy freight barges over to Keaunikakai Harbor on Molokai. They were great big things, twelve to fifteen feet high and several hundred feet long. When one was loaded, it held seventy-five head of cattle, heavy equipment, cars, and so forth. *The Rosa* was the name of this particular barge.

One day we set out and the weather was stormy. It was really choppy in the harbor. One tug pulled the barge over on a harness and a lead line and took it into the harbor where a smaller boat came out to tow it to shore. It was then that a cable snapped and *The Rosa* ran aground on a coral reef part way into the harbor. She was stuck tight and nothing would budge her. She was embedded but good!

Dillingham sent experts over from Honolulu and a helicopter flew in with a heavy loop-line about a hundred feet long. The barge had run aground with her lead line pointing into the reef and they hoped to attach the loop-line to the stern and pull her off backwards. But there were all kinds of problems.

The loop-line was so heavy that a pendulum effect was set up as it dangled from the 'copter and it started to swamp the craft before it could even reach the barge. The pilot was good however and every time it reached the end of the pendulum's swing, he would dip down and drop the line into the ocean to steady it.

One of the problems was how to get the cattle ashore. There was no feed or water on the barge and no way to get it to them as the closest a small craft was able to approach was a couple of hundred feet away. Then people would have to wade the rest of the way over the reef to the barge carrying the supplies. It looked as though it would be at least six or seven days until the next high tide and by then the cattle would be lost in the hot sun.

The final solution was ingenious! A Hawaiian cowboy was hired from a ranch on Molokai and a big net was hung from the helicopter. The cowboy cut out the cattle one at a time from the rest of the herd and rode them into the net in the water. The legs of the cattle poked through the net and the copter lifted each cow, net and all, safely to shore.

By this time, the high water mark on the barge was up above the water about six inches. It was high and dry. The plan was to attach the loop-line to the stern of the barge in order to fashion a harness, then attach a lead line to that so the tugs could pull it off. High tide was at midnight so they got hooked up and started pulling at nine. Nothing happened. They continued to pull. Ten o'clock came. Then eleven, twelve, one o'clock. High tide had come and gone and still nothing happened. The barge hadn't budged an inch. They continued to try the next day. They had set up site marks on the barge and tug to a point on the shore so that if the barge shifted even a fraction of a degree it would be detected. Nothing happened.

Later that afternoon we were sitting around the Hotel Molokai waiting for low tide to pass. It was our first hot meal in many days and there were a lot of local people there eating as well. Of course the talk centered on the barge and the plans to free it. Our head engineer was there. Suddenly one of the local people turned to him and said, "You aren't going to get nowhere doing it the *haole way!*"

"What do you mean the *haole way?*" he replied.

They then told him that if he really wanted to get that barge off that reef he had better honor the local customs. Well, by that time he was ready to try anything as nothing else had worked so far. So they got an old Hawaiian man from the island that was highly recommended, Uncle Somebody, and they took him out to the barge. He had some Hawaiian salt with him and a bunch of *ti* leaves. He climbed on board and started sprinkling salt all around. Then he took the *ti* leaves and tied them to the stern of the barge since that was the end they were going to tow. Then he chanted some Hawaiian words and proceeded to *shishi* (urinate) all around the barge. (I don't know what *that* was supposed to do, but that is what he did.)

It wasn't even high tide yet. It was a little early, but they got the tug and started the engines. I want to tell you that thing shot off of that reef like it was sitting on melted butter! It went as smooth and as quick as could be and it went fast! It went so fast that the tug reels couldn't handle it and the cable looped. It shot off that reef like greased lightning and they towed it back to Oahu.

Of course some people said that the barge would have come off the reef anyway. All I know is that nothing would budge it before. It was like trying to tow the island itself. But as soon as the Hawaiian way was initiated, it slipped off!

A Haunted Coffee Shack

Julius Scammon Rodman is a writer, scholar of Hawaiiana, and an anthropologist. Among his published works are *The Book of Hawaiian Tapas*; *Unending Melody, Memoirs of a Beachcomber;* and *The Kahuna Sorcerers of Hawaii, Past and Present*. A review of the latter title in the *Sunday Star-Bulletin* stated, "Rodman has woven a fascinating tangle of vignettes and portraits that literally boggle the mind and entice the intellect to stunning conjecture." Mr. Rodman lived for many years in Cloverfields, a historic mansion in Olympia, Washington.

Many people are fascinated by ghosts. They are not at all disturbed by the phenomena, but want to study it instead. They welcome the experience when it comes, watch very closely everything about it, and make notes on it. Now that's a very cool-headed person as far as I'm concerned.

Julius S. Rodman with his wife, Helen Eskridge, at Cloverfields in 1988.

I have written of a ghost experience I had in a haunted shack in Kalalau Valley on Kauai in my book, *The Kahuna Sorcerers of Hawaii, Past and Present*. However, I had another similar experience that took place on the Big Island that I didn't write about. It was at Keauhou before the great hotels and the golf course and the development of the harbor. There was a little circular cove there then, maybe two

Julius Scammon Rodman at his historic home, Cloverfields, in Olympia, Washington.

hundred yards across, and sometime the inter-island boats would stop there. Maybe five or six Hawaiian families lived there, although there had been fifty or more until the decline of the village in the 1930s. When I arrived, there were only five houses and several vacant ones scattered here and there.

During the 1930s, it was my practice to backpack when I was doing archaeology on the outer islands. I would walk mostly and ride now and then. I wouldn't have to hitchhike, as people were very hospitable; they would stop and ask me where I was going and offer me a ride. At that time, you could buy any old kind of a rattletrap, a Model-T, a touring car or a sedan of six or twelve cylinders, for about ten dollars. Now those old cars would cost from twenty to thirty thousand dollars today as they would be considered antiques, but then they were so plentiful and cheap that if a bearing wore out or if too many things went wrong, you could just drive them over a cliff or take them out into a cane field and leave them. There were masses of them all over the used car lots just waiting to be picked up. I would often buy one like that to use on an island for a week or so and then just leave it after pulling the yellow papers off. My trips were usually never more than two weeks.

I did freelance archeology during the 1930s, up until 1942. I just went out among the ruins—*heiaus* (temples), old house platforms—and picked up the old adzes, poi pounders, scrapers, and mica stones, whatever I could find. Hawaiians had them in their homes and often would just give them to me. I don't think I ever made a trip that I didn't have at least one poi pounder given to me. It was lonely work hiking around backpacking by yourself. The moment darkness came, what were you going to do with no TV, no radio, and no lamp to read a book, out there in the wilderness sleeping under a tree or in an empty house or church? I was always glad when there was a family nearby that I could visit with until it was time to go to sleep.

There was a Hawaiian family sitting out on their lanai this particular time at Keauhou. Several enormous Hawaiian women were sitting cross-legged on their mats, weaving *lauhala* and doing their work in the cool of the night. They were stripping *hala* and had the stuff lying all around in rolls and they were making various things out of it. They welcomed me and I sat down and talked with them until about 9:30.

I had picked out a deserted house to sleep in that night and I asked them about it. They said to go ahead as it had been deserted for many years. However, they said, "watch out for the spooks and the *aumakua* (protector spirits). All those old houses are haunted with ghosts in them, every one you know, so just watch out for the spirits!" Their warning provoked much laughter as I bid them goodnight and started for my place.

It was a typical Hawaiian country dwelling, an old coffee shack, the likes of which are seen all over the Islands. I had to beat down the brush to get to the front door, which had fallen down. There had been half a dozen stairs up to the front lanai of this one and they had all fallen down, so there were just a lot of boards laying all over the ground. I had to pull myself up chest high in order to get into the place so I threw my blanket and backpack in first. I pulled myself up in the darkness and after exploring four or five rooms made my way into a back bedroom with the aid of a flashlight. I lay down in a corner and was just dozing off when I heard a movement on the back porch (which, incidentally, was still intact). I heard a definite sound on this back lanai of footsteps, which came through the door and on into the kitchen, or what was left of it. These footsteps were accompanied by the sound of heavy breathing as though a very elderly person were having a breathing problem. All of this was accompanied by another distinct sound, that of a cane tapping very slowly: *tap, tap, tap.* The movements were so slow that it had to be either a very aged person or someone so sick that they weren't able to move very fast. I figured it would have to be an elderly person as young people rarely use canes. It took a long time for the footsteps and the tapping to cross that kitchen floor! I had my flashlight ready, but other than that I didn't know what I was going to do. I knew that I had to make up my mind in the minute or two that I had before the footsteps reached me as they were continuing steadily in my direction. What would happen when they got to me?

There was the normal night light in the room that you have in every house, even by the dark of the moon, so the general outline of the person crossing the room towards me should have been there. The sounds and the tapping continued to advance straight for me, however, I saw nothing. The person continued to advance through the doorway and across the floor to my corner. I had the flashlight in my hand and when the sounds were no more than ten feet from me, I suddenly turned it on and shot the beam to where the footsteps approached. There was a rapid shuffling as if feet were turning in confusion and a tapping all around. Then the tapping rapidly made retreat to the doorway from which it had entered as if the person were making a great effort to run from the middle of the room. When it reached the doorway (which held no door) and crossed the kitchen, I followed. I could hear the footsteps on the narrow little back porch and then a sort of crash in the bushes. I saw the bushes part and there was a movement of the *lantana* along with a crackling of the undergrowth for a moment, but...*there was nothing there at all.*

The next morning, I went back to see the Hawaiian family. When they asked how I had spent the night, I told them what had happened; about the footsteps and the tapping and the rest of it. They exchanged glances, but they didn't seem surprised.

"Oh," said the mother, "that's the old judge. He lived in that house for years. He walked with a cane and he breathed heavily. He died thirty years ago."

Night Visitors

I have had twenty or more night visitations since 1977. My first attack occurred a few minutes after 2 a.m. when I was awakened by a sensing of a very menacing presence in the bedroom. I actually felt a sensation approaching terror. It was terrifying in the supernatural sense and not a friendly thing at all.

I'm a timer and have a lifelong habit of looking at my watch when things happen and noting the time. It was interesting that every one of these visitations happened between 2 and 3 o'clock in the morning and usually right after two. Curiously enough, I was always lying on my back as well.

Seconds after sensing this sinister presence in the corner of my room, I had the feeling that it had crossed over and was at the foot of my bed. Then a curious silent vibration hovered over my feet like a motor giving off waves of energy. It was suspended maybe six inches over me and it made no noise. The vibrations hit against my legs and touched my feet, then began to move slowly up my legs. When it reached my pelvic region, I threw up the covers and sat up suddenly. I had had enough of it!

There was nothing more. I didn't see a thing. There was some phase of the moon that night and I could see everything very clearly in the twilight of my room. I could even see my books on the other side of my bed, but I could see nothing that could have caused the vibration.

The thing took many different forms after that first visit. Sometimes it came as a pressure snuggled into my side like a very large cat about eighteen inches long. It would press up against me like a soft animal and if I moved just a little bit, it would push up against me even more. I could define its presence as I always pinched myself to make sure I was awake. If I moved strongly enough, it would be gone for the night and it wouldn't come back until another night.

Sometimes it would come as a presence—always between 2 and 3 a.m.—which would jerk the covers inch by inch up or down or maybe sideways until I would finally yell and throw my arms up. Then it would stop. Sometimes it would pull them halfway off and sometimes it would pull them totally off and throw them on the floor. One night I was awakened by two strong hands gripping my ankles, which gave my body a violent jerk, that seemed to pull me down towards the foot of the bed. It was such a jolt that my teeth clicked together.

At first I couldn't speak. It was as if my voice was frozen and I couldn't make a sound. Finally, with great effort, I could overcome the block in my larynx and, summoning all my forces, I began to make whole phrases. I would say, "Who are you?" or "What do you want?" or "Stop! Go away!" and even "What the hell do you want?" As soon as I would speak, it would go away. It was as if I could command it to leave.

In the first two years of these occurrences, they came every three or four months. I should have put down the dates. I meant to do that and I even got a pad out at one time. I don't know why I didn't keep a detailed record of it all, but I didn't.

It had been several months since I had had a visitation until last week (October 1, 1986). All I had experienced for the previous nine months was a little cover pulling. Last week, I awakened by the sensation of some indescribable force gripping my right foot and seeming to charge it with an almost electric energy. I instantly yelled and kicked and shook my leg vigorously and the sensation went right away from the foot. This sensation defies description... *as if IT comes from another plane*.

Several months ago I got a copy of David Hufford's *The Terror that Comes in the Night.* I think he is talking of the same visitations that I have experienced, but almost none of the score or more methods of attack upon my person are described in his book and no similar case histories are cited. According to Hufford, one-sixth of the population has experienced similar nighttime occurrences. Hufford indicates that these visitations occur when the subject is lying on their back and I noted that every one of my episodes took place when I was on my back.

I can only tell you that this has been my experience.

The Ghost in the Nursery

Kim (Dave) Warrington was an architectural designer and contractor from Martha's Vineyard, Massachusetts. He has worked with many famous people during the course of his career, including former First Lady Jackie Kennedy and movie star Doris Day.

We moved into the house the night before Hurricane Eva hit Oahu. It was a beautiful million-dollar "shack" on Kailua Beach. My girlfriend, Tera, my two sons, Jamie and Chris, and I had agreed to housesit for the owner who was on a trip to the mainland. She was a widow and she was flying her oldest son back to Yale where he was a freshman.

The house was built around a big swimming pool. The master bedroom was in one corner and next to it was obviously the kids' wing with bunk beds and a toy box still filled with old games and books. A long hallway went all around the pool on the inside of the house. It was an elegant place with expensive furnishings. Although it was too fancy for my personal taste, it was great fun to be in such a setting for a time. The woman was wealthy and active in the Honolulu Symphony and the walls of her study were covered with personally autographed photos and letters from famous people: Luciano Pavarotti, Eugene Ormandy, people like that. The bed in the master bedroom was an unbelievable creation of swathed satin of the palest blue so fine that we were afraid to touch it, much less sit on it. The room was sumptuous and beautifully decorated, yet there was something strange about it. It was always cold in there, at least ten degrees below the temperature of the rest of the house.

Actually, the whole house felt funny and we all picked up on it although nobody said anything at the time. At first, Jamie and Chris didn't want to sleep in the room with the bunk beds, but when we told them it would be their room while we were staying there, they agreed.

We had barely moved in when Hurricane Eva was due to hit the island. We just had time to nail a piece of plywood over the huge glass picture window overlooking the beach when a hala tree blew into it. If we hadn't put the board up in time, we would have had smashed glass all over the living room.

Of course the electricity went out all along the beachfront. It was out in our area for over a week. We had made a trip to Star Market for groceries as soon as we heard the storm was coming, so we were okay.

We managed to weather the hurricane although it was the experience of a lifetime. The wind howled like the fiends of hell unleashed and being plunged into pitch darkness with only candles to light added to the eeriness of the time. We all huddled together in blankets, built a fire in the fireplace, told stories, sang songs, and tried to make a picnic of it.

After the storm, we spent the next few days cleaning up the yard and fishing palm branches out of the swimming pool. We were without electricity the entire eight days we stayed in the house. When it got dark, we continued to light candles and since there wasn't much else to do, we all went to bed early. That's when things started to happen.

At first we didn't think too much about it when we began to hear noises in rooms that were totally empty when we went to investigate. Then we noticed that doors would close by themselves. Well, there were trade winds, we said, circulating through the house, right? But then we noticed that when we closed the door to the guest room, it would be open the next time we passed. We knew that the kids hadn't been in that wing of the house. Strangest of all, we noticed that although the electricity had been off since the storm and all of the water in the house was stone cold and had been for three days, the water in the master bath was piping hot! And so it remained for the rest of the week even though there was neither electricity nor solar heat. Even though we could not explain that, we still didn't think anything really amiss although we couldn't put our finger on why we all felt so uncomfortable in the place.

It was on the third night that it happened. We had put the boys to bed in the nursery right after dark and Tera and I had been enjoying the fireplace in the living room. We had a drink or two and were pooped from cleaning up the yard. Tera had fallen asleep on the couch. I had shaken her to tell her I was going to bed and for her to come too. I had carefully removed the satin bedspread and was lying in bed waiting for her when I saw a figure walk by the bedroom door and go towards the nursery. I was drowsy and automatically thought it was Tera in a long white robe going down the hall to check on the boys before coming to bed. I waited at least ten minutes for her to join me, but she didn't come. I was beginning to get annoyed and wondered what the hell she was doing. Was she playing some kind of game or was there something the matter with the kids? I got up out of bed and lit a candle to walk into the boys' room to see what was happening. Chris and Jamie were sound asleep in the bunk beds and Tera was nowhere in sight.

Now there was one other bedroom past the nursery with a connecting door, but no way out from there. There was a backdoor at the end of the house, but it was bolted shut and had not been touched. I checked both doors, which were shut tight. The other bedroom was empty. At this point I began to panic. I thought perhaps a prowler had gained entry because *I knew I had seen someone walk down the hall.*

I quickly went back to the living room and there was Tera sound asleep on the couch where I had left her. I had forgotten she was wearing blue jeans and didn't own a long white robe or dressing gown. I woke her up and asked if she had just been down the hall to check on the boys. She gave me a blank look and said she hadn't budged. It was then that the hair on the back of my neck stood up on end and I said 'aueeeee, something's happening!' We both combed the entire house and there was no one there. Everything was in order.

We stayed in the house for eight days in all. The electricity never did come back on and we were busy trying to save the expensive cuts of beef in the freezer (we didn't) and keep things running as best we could.

I had several vivid impressions during those last few days. Just before falling asleep the night after glimpsing the figure in the hall, I had a flash that a man was standing next to the boys with his hands in his pockets, just looking down at them watching them sleep. When I got up and checked their room, no one was there and I told myself my imagination was running away with me. Then I noticed pictures in the den of the owner, I presumed, with his two young sons taken several years before. Both boys looked remarkably like my sons, Chris and Jamie, and appeared in the photographs to be about the same ages. I was especially taken with one photo of a young tall vigorous man with his arms around each boy. They werc smiling into the camera and you could almost sense the love and devotion he felt for his kids from the picture.

After a week, we had an opportunity to rent a cottage in Lanikai. Although we hadn't talked about it, none of us could wait to get out of that house. We packed our things and vacated as soon as possible. I couldn't help but wonder about the habitual chill in the nursery wing and about the fact that after eight days without electricity, the water in the master bedroom was still piping hot.

It all began to fall into place about three weeks later when our neighbor came to visit. She had previously been a house sitter in the Kailua mansion and was the one responsible for our week spent there during the hurricane. Somehow the conversation turned to the house and how uncomfortable we all were staying in it. Now this was an older lady as tough as a boot from New England, but she admitted that the reason she had wanted to get out of the place was because she had felt so darned uncomfortable the entire time she had been there. She thought that maybe it had something to do with the fact that the father had died in the house!

That stopped me, and I asked her to repeat what she had just said. She then related how the father had been a vigorous athletic man who had adored his two young blond sons. They had all lived in the Kailua Beach house until he had been stricken with an illness that he knew would be fatal. His boys were just Chris and Jamie's ages when he became sick. Although he knew he was dying, he refused to go to the hospital and insisted on staying at home during the extremely long and excruciating illness. After eight months, he died in bed in the master bedroom. This had all happened about five years before.

The boys were almost identical in appearance to my two sons at the same age. The bunk beds in the nursery had belonged to them. The mother had continued to raise the boys in the same house until she left to accompany the older son to college. Hence the need for a house-sitter. Our friend was so uncomfortable that she talked us into taking her place.

Although I had never believed in ghosts before, I *KNEW* I had *SEEN* someone walk down the hall.

I think the father was just not ready to let go.

A Brush with Pele

Dennis Keawe is an artist and craftsman in the old Hawaiian traditions. An expert in tapa making, he has taught and demonstrated his art through Bishop Museum. He lives on the Big Island of Hawaii.

It has always been said that Pele's dog will appear before a major eruption of the volcano. If you happen to come across a big white dog out in the middle of nowhere, that's likely to be Pele's dog.

I came across a white dog while traveling across the lava fields one day. It looked like a white German shepherd. Big! I had some Honolulu people with me, one from the Leeward Community College and a Pearl Harbor worker. I slowed the truck down and stopped right next to the dog.

"Huuuuuuiiiiiiiiiiiiiii? You want to come with us?" I said.

Well, it just stands there. I tell my two friends, "Hey, guess whose dog this is, eh?"

Aieeeeeee! The next day the volcano blew up! We were almost inundated by lava from that Mauna Loa flow. Everybody was getting very nervous. Pele's dog is almost always a portent of what's to come, I think.

And then there is the Puna Cave. Legend says this cave has the picture of the vagina of Pele's sister on the floor of it. I have seen it. In fact, I have gone into it. I was one of the first to be admitted before it was opened to the public. It was discovered in 1982 by spelunkers, cave explorers from the Mainland. They had heard about a cave of this sort and sure enough they stumbled right across it.

It is remarkable. The entire cave is black lava. Now everyone thinks of a cave as being tubular and circular. This cave, if you can imagine, goes on a semi-circular cross section with a flat floor and a vaulted semi-circular ceiling. Most caves have irregular brownish-black lava. This cave is black all around with one startling feature: on the floor is an incredible natural formation of brilliant red lava that appears to be a double labia fold. The floor of the cave spreads in both directions to flare up from the right and left flanks for all the world symbolic of "legs"—parted legs at that. If you go down either side or "leg," there is another cave just underneath that is like an anal opening. It's one of the most amazing things I have ever seen!

A Ghost at Puna

Leslie Fergussen is a newcomer—a malahini—to Maui from the mainland. She worked as a waitress at a major hotel on the Kaanapali strip for two years.

When I first came to Maui, I moved into a subdivision in Puna. I had a roommate named Kim who was the only girl in her family and used to getting anything she wanted. When we first went to look at the place, it was odd for her not to want the bedroom with the bath. It was definitely the nicest room. When I asked her why she didn't take it for herself, she replied that she didn't like the vibes. I checked out the room and said no problem, it feels okay to me and I moved in.

The first night I was alone in the house. I had come home so tired from work that I had gone straight to bed and was reading a book. I was alcohol free and everything. All of a sudden, I felt as if a big party were going on in the room. I didn't see anything and I didn't hear a sound, but I *felt* all of these presences. I said to myself, hey, am I going crazy or what? I tried to shake off the feeling by getting up and moving around. When I did that, the feeling dissipated and finally went away completely. I felt better and went back to bed. I had no sooner picked up my book, however, when here *IT* came again. There was an intense feeling of commotion in the airwaves and a whole bunch of something really going to it and doing their thing! It was like a big invisible party with a lot of invisible people. I said no way, that's it! I got up to get out of there and that's when I got hurt.

I don't like to remember it. It gives me "chicken skin" just to think about it. I got to the top of the stairs and that's when I felt his hand on the back of my neck. I know it was a male hand and he was young. It was not an old man's hand. It was as real as anything. I will remember it all my life and no one will ever convince me that it didn't happen.

He grabbed the back of my neck hard and gave me a shove and pushed me down the stairs. I fell and sprained my wrist. I had to wear a brace and I had bruises and scratches all over for weeks. For a while I was unable to use my right hand at work.

Well, that did it! I wouldn't go back into that room again, much less sleep there. I asked my roommate if I could share her bedroom (because she wouldn't set foot in there either) and we did for a while. I was afraid that people would think we were a couple of lesbians, but I couldn't tell anyone the truth. I didn't want them to think I was crazy. Who would believe I had a ghost—or maybe a lot of ghosts—in my bedroom?

When I first moved into the room, I discovered a door to a closet that was locked. Now I wasn't about to live in a house with a locked closet when I didn't know what was inside, so I managed to get it open. I found an old trunk in there. It was really old and filled with yellowed photographs of businesses in Maui that were no longer there, old newspaper clippings and old books with pieces of lace inserted between some of the pages, that kind of thing. Nothing spectacular, just a bunch of old stuff that someone had put in there a long time ago. I don't know, of course, but just maybe the old trunk had something to do with the activity in that room.

2

Kupuna Make A'ole Loa

Hawaii's Elders Never Die

Introduction

My earliest memories are of Hawaii. Although I was not born in the Islands nor am I of Hawaiian lineage, it is my home. Over the years, I had many opportunities to meet and to know some of Hawaii's luminaries, or personalities, who in one way or another contributed greatly to the magic of the Islands.

While just a toddler, I remember peering into the dark shimmering waters of the *koi* pond amidst the orchids and bamboo of The Willows Restaurant. Alan McGuire, treasurer of the *Honolulu Advertiser*, and his wife Mary Ann were my godparents and it was Alan's mother, Mrs. Hausten, who began the legendary restaurant in Makiki. Years later, I was privileged to interview Hannah "Nana" Veary over luncheon there.

I remember taking painting lessons at the Honolulu Academy of Art with Jon Young and, again years later, exhibiting beside him in the Ala Moana Art Festival. Another Island painter, Jean Charlot, was gracious enough to autograph the books he illustrated for each one of my children, which they treasure to this day. Henry Blakstad, a *kaimaaina* who grew up in the house at Punaluu (which later became the Crouching Lion

Judi Thompson, composer Alex Anderson, and Rebecca Thompson at the 1984 Na Makua Mahalo Ia Awards Ceremony, Brigham Young University-Hawaii Campus. Anderson wrote "Lovely Hula Hands" and "Mele Kalikimaka" among many other popular songs.

Restaurant), became a major Charlot collector and we shared many a dinner in his tiny, elegant apartment amidst his million-dollar art collection stacked against the walls. Arthur and Kathryn Murray lived directly upstairs from Henry and it was there in their penthouse overlooking Waikiki beach that Mr. Murray asked, "Do you like to dance?" I was so nervous to be dancing with ARTHUR MURRAY that I immediately stepped on his foot. He threw back his head and laughed, "If you only knew how many feet I've stepped on, but nobody says a thing because *I'm Arthur Murray!*" We danced many times after that and now I feel prepared to dance with the President of the United States.

So many vignettes stand out like jewels in memory: training under Olympic Swim Coach Clarence Sakamoto during my freshman year at University of Hawaii; learning hula from the

Beamers as a co-ed during summer session there; enjoying Ten-Boy Shrimp Curry dinner at the Foods of the Pacific cooking class with Katharine Bazore, who wrote the book; taking yet another memorable cooking class with Titus Chan at Moilili Community Center; escorting legendary songwriter Alex Anderson to the Na Makua Mahalo Ia ceremony at Brigham Young University-Hawaii Campus to accept his award for his many beloved compositions including the seasonal and still popular "Mele Kalikimaka." My daughter Rebecca and I were entertained during the long drive from Honolulu to the North Shore by his fascinating tales of World War I, the Red Baron, and being shot down behind enemy lines as I tried to reconcile this charming silver-haired gentleman with "Lovely Hula Hands" and "The Cockeyed Mayor of Kaunakakai." Escorting another Island Great, Winona Beamer, to Katharine Luomala's book party for *Hula Ki'i: Hawaiian Puppetry* so she could perform a real *hula ki'i* to honor the author; meditating with Nana Veary at her home in Aina Haina and the many happy times with her sharing pie, tea, and wonderful stories at the Yum Yum Tree in Kahala Mall; and later working as an editor with so many Hawaiian scholars at the Institute for Polynesian Studies, including Edith MacKinzie and her Hawaiian Genealogies series; June Gutmanis' *Pohaku;* Ishmael Stagner's *HULA*; and Dr. Rubelite Johnson.

And I will never forget Senator Hiram Fong waiting to greet our busload of Hale Kipa Home for Runaway Students in order to personally show them around his lovely botanical gardens in Kaneohe. It was the first time many of them had been out of Honolulu and the first field trip they had ever experienced. We had prepared by reading his Horatio Alger life story biography as the first Asian politician to go to Washington D.C. and had seen his photo before driving over the Pali to meet with the man himself. The dozen teenagers from difficult and often devastating backgrounds were thunderstruck to have this famous man take the time to escort them through his park in a tour they would never forget.

Unforgettable as well was the personal tour by Richard Marks, sheriff and former patient at Kalaupapa Leper Colony on Molokai before it was turned into a national park. Driving like a mad man, he kept us spellbound with his stories as we bounced about like popcorn in his old station wagon over the rut-filled road to Father Damien's church perched on the most rugged and breathtaking cliff-lined coast in the world.

And then there were quiet times enjoyed such as the hours spent listening to ghost stories in the sun on June Gutmanis' *lanai* (porch or patio) tucked in back of her North Shore sugar-shack banana-grove home, pure Island, all charm. And the visit to Auntie Harriet Ne in Molokai as she entranced us with her encounters with Night Marchers, Menehune, and Mu. And Inez Ashdown in Maui with her marvelous recollections of Queen Liliuokalani and her personal *akua*, the *pueo*, the white owl.

It goes on and on and on. Remember the quip, "If I'd known I was living through an era, I would have paid more attention"? Luckily, I paid enough attention to collect the following stories. I just wish I had gotten more...

Judi Thompson
San Miguel de Allende, Mexico
June 13, 2008

Inez Ashdown Remembers

Inez MacPhee Ashdown was born in 1899 and came to Maui in 1907. She was a journalist and teacher, and has authored many books including *Stories of Old Lahaina*; *Mystical Molokai, Many Legends, Much History*; *Kealaloa O Maui, Kaho'olawe*; and *Cradle of the Faith*. She has served as a Maui County Historic Sites Commissioner, County Historian, and Kamehameha Day Parade Grand Marshall. She graciously welcomed us to her home on Maui in 1984 to share her experiences.

Early Days in Wyoming

My father was an old Wyoming man and, my gosh, where could you find a more wonderful place for spirits and Indian stories than Wyoming? Our old house back in Cheyenne was haunted. It was my grandfather's place. He went out to Wyoming in the early 1860s as an officer in the Calvary. I was born at Camp Collins, Fort D.A. Russell. It's now called Fort Warren where they have an Air Force base named for one of the governors, which angered me. Why don't they name it for the old army officers? My grandfather built every red brick building that's on the post.

I was born there, but my mother and I lived in several houses while my father was in the Spanish American War. We bought one of these houses and put it up in what was then a "tent city," later Nineteenth and Wheel Streets in Cheyenne. It was a two-storied house and it was haunted. Somebody had been killed there in the old days, or so the story went. You could sit quietly in the kitchen or in what they called the parlor where the piano was kept, and you could hear sounds of footsteps going up the stairs. This happened at certain times, supposedly the date of the killing.

Then there was the west bedroom. I wouldn't sleep in that room for anything you would give me, but my Uncle Ned would and he used to hear things. One night something snatched the covers off and it scared him. He yelled, "Who came up and snatched my bedclothes off?"—if anybody did or not. Several times he had experiences of that kind and we thought it was—how do you call that thing—poltergeist? Maybe it was one of those. Oh, there are all kinds of stories like that I've learned.

The two back rooms in my grandfather's house were supposed to be haunted. He had all of his Calvary stuff in there with his keepsakes and his desk. I used to go in there to get a saber to play with. We kids had a "dungeon" down in the cellar and in order to have lights down there so we could see, we took candles and put them on the ends of bayonets and stuck them in the walls. Oh, we were real soldiers then! Of course, if we were Indians, we didn't have that and we took that away. We always cleaned the bayonets very well indeed so they wouldn't rust, because Grampa would have given us the devil if we didn't.

Out there on those prairies eighty miles from nowhere, you sure could hear ghost stories. We lived a life of... not make-believe, really—but you walked with an *aumakua* or a guardian angel or whatever. I don't care what you call it. If you really believe in it, it walks beside you and it will protect you. The only time that mine didn't protect me, Poppa saved me.

My dog and I had this old flea-bitten grey horse named Pegasus and I used to ride him. There was a creek in the meadow not far from the house and the animals would come to drink there, sometimes mountain lions, sometimes coyotes, sometimes other things used to come in the summertime. You didn't see much of it in the winter, although the wolves would come then. (I knew a fox terrier that was always running after chipmunks by the creek there.) Well, I was going along on Pegasus that day, having a fine time when a black and white dog came along. I ran to get it and, you know, it wasn't a dog. It was a skunk! My guardian angel wasn't there that day. Poppa met me on the way home. My mother buried my clothes. She took all kinds of soap and washed the dog and me. My skin burned from being washed, but it didn't do any good until it wore off.

Johnny Lick was my *kahu* (caretaker) out there on the ranch in Wyoming. He was part Indian and part Dutch. There was an old wolf called "Old Three Legs." It had been in a trap at one time and had chewed its own foot off to get free. You could tell he was old because of his color. He used to kill calves on the ranch. One day Johnny shot the wolf and made it into a rug. I used to sit on that rug in front of the fireplace and read *Grimms Fairy Tales*, *The Scottish Chiefs*, and all the little *Beatrix Potter* books. How I loved them. I was reading them all the way over to the Hawaiian Islands on board the *USS Alameida* with my mother sick in the stateroom and all the passengers seasick except Poppa and me. I would read those stories to Poppa and to the Captain up on the bridge. They allowed me to do that. That's the kind of thing a child can remember that gives beauty to life as you grow older. You keep these experiences in your book of memories, they sustain you and you're not afraid. There's no use being afraid because God always is with you if you talk to Him, you know.

We Come to Hawaii

My mother and father and I came to Hawaii in January of 1908. Poppa had just come down as champion roper of the world from the Wyoming Frontier Days as a guest of the Territorial government and he decided to return to the ranch at Hamakua after he was offered the position of manager. He went over to the Big Island with Egan and the rest of the boys from Wyoming, while Mom and I went on to Hamakua. It so happened that Queen Liliuokalani and her party were going into Lahaina. We arrived together and that is when I first met the Queen. We stayed a time and then we all went on to the ranch where Poppa took over as manager from Dr. Raymond and his wife. The previous owners, Captain James Makee and his wife, were buried in the mausoleum on Pukukikia, right there on the ranch.

One night Poppa went down to Makena and took two of the cowboys along with him as escort. He worked with them and they were all friends. Now my mother was a very strange person. She had kind of a second-sight sort of thing, as she was "born with a veil." Some of her family came out of Ireland and you know how they are about "ghosties." There was a white picket fence around the house and late that night, Momma woke up when she heard somebody slam the gate. Then she heard footsteps coming up the walk and onto the lanai. When she heard the front door slam, she called out, "Angus, is that you?" But no one answered. I was sleeping in the old Captain's bedroom and I heard her call out. Now Momma was from Wyoming where you were liable to run into a renegade Indian or a bad man off the railroad tracks or a hobo anytime, so immediately she went to get somebody up there. She called on Mokano, the cook, who had the guns. He wouldn't come out of his house, but he finally pacified her by firing a gun into the air.

Now all this time things were walking and she heard all of these footsteps and nobody was there. She had lit all the lamps when Mokano finally told her, "Missus, you go sleep. No use you walk around like this because tonight is the anniversary of Captain Makee's death. Each time, he come walk in his house. He come look over what the people are doing now!"

Of course, when Poppa heard about it the next day, he said everybody's crazy and he doesn't believe in that kind of thing. But Momma did. And all this time, I'm sleeping in the Captain's bedroom.

I Meet the Captain in His Tomb

There was an old mausoleum on the ranch where Captain James Makee and his wife were buried. I used to go down and sit on top of it when I was a little girl. I guess it was 1909 when somebody came along and broke the iron doors of the tomb and went into it. Of course, with Poppa being the manager, word of what happened reached him immediately and we all went down there on our horses. Although the main doors were bolted, the iron doors were open. We went inside and I won't ever forget what we saw.

The lids were off the coffins. Captain Makee and his wife were right there. Evidently they had been embalmed. I remember a statue of a soldier back in front of the capital building in Cheyenne. It was made of grey granite, and that's what these two people looked like. There was a scar on his face. The Captain had been assaulted by one of his crewmembers coming out of Lahaina once and the scar was still there. Their clothes were kind of green. Of course, the Makee family came and took them away and put them in Nuuanu, where they rest today. *But his ghost didn't leave*. He stayed on at old Hamakua. It's a lovely story. I still delight in it.

I believe in Captain Makee. I think the reason the old house finally burned down is because Captain Makee did it. This is how deep it goes with me. The ranch was not taken care of as he and my father cared for it, and the rest before us. I was in the hospital when somebody from the *Honolulu Advertiser* called me and said, "Did you used to live at old Hamakua? It just burned down!" I dang near had another heart attack! Why did he tell me like that? I always thought that Captain Makee burned that house down because he loved it with all his heart and so did his wife. I felt that I knew them because I saw them in their coffins. The Captain never hurt anybody, but he was there. All these things, you know, make a big impression on a child growing up.

Memories of Queen Lilioukalani

My Momma and I didn't want to come to the Hawaiian Islands ignorant so we got out our history books and we studied about Hawaii before we arrived here so that we knew a little bit. When I got here I learned the word "Aloha," and Queen Liliuokalani loved me. She would come sometimes to Punahou School and we would go up to Manoa for a ride in her carriage. She had a Negro footman. He must have been Hawaiian, but he was very dark so I thought he was a Negro coachman like my grandfather had back in Wyoming. She was the first one to tell me the story of that rocky hill in back of Punahou. In those days there was nothing much back in the valley and it was magnificent with all of those beautiful rainbows. She used to tell me, "Those rainbows, they are for you and for me. We are *ali'i* (Hawaiian royalty)." She included me as an *ali'i* and I felt very proud. I was her little *hanai aloha* or child adopted in love. She told me the story of the waters of Manoa, of the *mo'o* who was the grandmother of the little children of the rainbow and how she became the rain of Manoa when she died. It was a lovely story.

She told me, "Don't forget the *Iolani,* the bird of Hawaii, and the golden eagle, the bird of the United States of America. The *Hai Hawaii*, the flag of the islands and the stars and stripes fly over us to protect us. Always be loyal."

She had no hatred. She had nothing like that in her heart and I thought that she surely must have. I thought that maybe Governor Dole and Governor Frear were her real enemies. I didn't know in those days. I was only seven years old.

One time, I was at a grand party and I was going through the receiving line. Governor Dole was in the line with the queen and others. He was a very tall handsome man. When I came to him, the queen said, "This is Governor Dole," and I put my hands behind my back and didn't make a curtsey.

"My dear," she said, "you're being very rude! Why are you acting this way? Greet Governor Dole. He's one of my best friends."

Well, that slayed me. She told us later that if it hadn't been for Governor Dole and a few more of the level-headed ones during the overthrow of the monarchy, she and Prince Kuhio might have been shot with the mob rushing around the way it did. (Prince Kuhio died when I was twenty-two.)

She told me not to blame the Americans for all this. It was Hawaiians, it was Chinese, and Japanese, and all kinds of merchants and people who turned on her (although not so much those on the plantations). She wanted a constitution of full power like King Kamehameha the First had and the people wouldn't stand for that. They were scared to death she could take away their land that they worked and that was one of her things. She wanted to let opium in as well as liquor in order to get the so-called duty out of it and those were two of her things. Queen Emma ran for office against King Kalakaua and the Emmaties were very unkind. I don't know what the queen was like, but some of her adherents who voted for her said some awful things about the Kalakaua family and David Kalakaua in particular. But it was more than that I know. I remember the day Queen Lilioukalani told me about that time. Tears came into her eyes that her own people had hurt her, you see.

All of these things I've lived and all of these things I know. Now today I tell others what Queen Liliuokalani taught my parents and me. In the Hawaiian language, every letter—a, e, i, o, u, and so on—has meaning. Kuilima—I—that is the basis of the language. That is the basis of all things. The meaning of ALOHA for instance. You take the letter A in ALOHA and that is fire, light, intelligence, and knowledge. All of those things come with the letter A or AH. The letter O is to the earth. LO would be female as LO is to the earth. All of this equals HA, the breath of God. When he creates, he breathes on the seeds. ALOHA. God is in you and in me and in everything he has ever created. That is how I've lived my life, as in the word, ALOHA. And I've taught this.

Queen Liliuokalani died when I was seventeen. I kept the doll that she gave me for my eighth birthday in Honolulu. Every time I get a chance I always go up to the Royal Cemetery in Nuuanu because Liliuokalani and so many that I knew are there. I don't much care to stay in the city, but I had read in the library that there was a *heiau* down in the gulch below the Royal Mausoleum. So the last time I was in Honolulu, I thought I would go and take a look. I felt maybe I could find it and I had nothing else to do, so I walked. I walked a long way and when I came to a certain place, I thought, "This is it!" But when I looked around I realized that time and so much water pouring down changes things and I could see nothing to recognize as a landmark. Yet I knew that this was where the *heiau* had been. I went up a little further and there was a trail solid up like a sculpture. I climbed up and found myself by the Royal Mausoleum. Bill Taylor was the caretaker at that time. He was standing there and asked me where I had come from up the hill like that.

"I'm looking for the *heiau*," I replied, "and it was right down there, wasn't it?"

"Yes, why?" he said.

I told him I had read about it and although there was nothing left of it, I knew it had been there. He put his arm around me.

"How long since you've been in the Mausoleum?"

"Long time."

He gave me a long look. "I'm going to take you down to visit Queen Liliuokalani and the rest," he said quietly.

We took a few flowers we picked out of a garden there and I said a prayer for her and the rest of them.

They're all dead. They're all gone. And yet sometimes I wonder... Why did a little girl from Wyoming come all the way to Hawaii? The queen said to me when we arrived, "You will stay in my land all your life. Help my people."

That stayed in my head, I felt knighted. I used to take the little doll and go walking and think of it.

An Aumakua for our Family

There was a little *heiau* on the side of the hill where the *pueo*, the owls, used to come. In Hawaii the owl is a god. If *pueo* comes to tell you that something bad is going to happen, you would pray to God for strength. Whatever is coming Dear God, I'll accept it, but please give me strength. You would pray like that.

When I had done something I wasn't supposed to (like ride a horse my father had said I shouldn't ride), I would go there for comfort because the owls were always there. I would always go there when I had been naughty. One day I had been rude and disobedient and Momma had had to switch my legs. I think I refused to do my lessons. Momma used to teach me daily, and every six weeks or so we would go to Punahou in Honolulu where Miss Winnie would prepare my lessons. My uncle and aunt had a place on King Street and I used to ride my horse on the government trails. So anyway, that was my little temple.

I was down there on this particular day when an owl came and sat right beside me. I looked at him and he didn't fly away or anything. I said to him, "I'm so sorry that I was naughty and had to be whipped!" and he made soothing sounds. I think if he had made a bad sign or scratched me I would have died. The owls were my friends, they were gods, see. That's what my *kahu* taught me.

Many years later when my youngest son went to the war in Korea as a pilot, he was coming home the night before he left for overseas. He was coming along toward Haakea Stream from Lahaina and he found an owl. He told me the next morning, "Mom, I found an owl last night and put him in the meat safe. You take care of him, okay?" When I heard that I felt funny inside. What does this mean?

I fed the owl and we got Jimmy off on the plane. Then I called my old friend Aupainui Kikahuna who lived over at Wailua. I had asked him at one time to give my son the *aumakua* of the *mana*. He said, "I cannot. Only God can give you." So when Jimmy found the owl the way he did at the owl cave area I knew there was something.

When I told Alapai what had happened, he said he'd be right over. He was just out of the hospital at the time and was not well, but they carried him over in the car. Two carloads of his Hawaiian family came over to pray thanks that God had given us the strongest *aumakua* of all. And I felt so good. The old man said, "Your son will come home. Don't worry about him, but he will be hurt because the owl has been hurt on his head."

Sure enough, when Jimmy came home he was hurt, a psychiatric thing. He had been squadron commander and President Truman had ordered his squadron to go out and drop napalm on a village in Korea. When Jimmy and some of his men went back to that village afterwards and saw what they had done, it pretty near put them all crazy. They didn't realize what napalm would do to that whole place, but they had to obey orders. To this day, he still can't get over it. And that's how he was hurt.

Charles, my husband, and I were going home to Kilohana and the ranch where I used to live with the Von Kepplers one night. We were driving up Puulawe Road when he stopped the car and got out. There's an owl on the road, he said. I picked it up and it was covered with blood. That gave me a funny feeling, but I prayed, "God help me to be strong. Whoever had died or got in an accident, please help them and help me. Help us all!"

I wrapped the owl in a newspaper and put him on my lap until we got home. Then I put him in a box with soft gauze and all. There was no use doing anything else as he was dying, but at least he could die in comfort and safety.

The next morning my son in Texas called. His wife had had a miscarriage and almost died on the operating table the night before.

I know that God gives us signs. He gives us things to help us. He gives us things to warn us. I believe in *aumakua*. I know *pueo* is the *aumakua* of our family because Alapai said so.

Pele and the Ranch at Hamakua

My father used to tell me all kinds of stories about Pele. I love Pele. Of course, as you know, there is only one God and no other, but spirits DO exist. Pele, to my mind, is the poetical imaginary idea the Hawaiian people had of a manifestation of the Creator. At the same time it's delightful to think of her as an old grizzle-haired woman. My *kahu* used to say, "Now you take care! You meet somebody very old, you be very polite. It might be Pele!"

Once there was a bad drought on the ranch and everybody was praying for rain. There was a *tiki,* a rain god, in the garden—it's still there—and people were putting leis on it and making offerings, but no rain came. What the heck good is a rain god unless it brings rain? There was Hina, a goddess, and Lono, the name of the god himself, and they were all praying to Lono. There was just a little water left in the fountain with goldfish in it and I didn't want to take their water. I walked up to the house where we had a spring and I got a little water. I walked back down to the rain god and threw the water in both of his faces, shouting, "NOW make it rain!"

I immediately felt sorry for what I had done, but I wouldn't apologize so I got on my horse bareback and started down the road, Kanaio side. I was almost to the place called Waiakahiliu when I remembered the story that was told about that spot.

It seemed that Pele had walked through that very place to test the people who lived there. She became very angry because they were all selfish. None of them would give her water from their gourds. None but one woman and she gave, saying, "Here Mother, take my gourd. Drink. You are old and you need help. You are welcome to it."

The old woman drank every drop and the people laughed except for that one woman. All of a sudden, the earth shook. The people all fell to their knees. It was Pele, but she wasn't old and grizzled this time. She was big and beautiful and wonderful and it scared the heck out of them, I suppose.

Anyway I started for this spring as it wasn't too far and I had nothing else to do. I was crossing the lava fields when along came a black dog. Then I remembered the part of the story that told about when the woman was wondering what to do for water and how far to walk. A black dog had come and shook himself and some of the water flew into her mouth. The water wasn't salty and so she followed him. When she got to a beautiful place, there was a spring of fresh clear water in the middle of the new lava flow.

Well, here comes this black dog and my horse, Southwind, began sniffing the air and prancing along the old grey ribbon trail. Pretty soon we got to the water and there it was. We drank and there was no more dog there. The dog had gone. Of course to me it was Poki, the dog of Pele.

I love these things, you know!

The Haunting Cane

The cane is displayed in the old Bailey House, *Hale o Kahuku*, which is now a museum in Wailuku. There is a sign on it that says simply, "Haunting Cane." It's not haunted though. It haunts things. A haunting cane.

I'll tell you about the cane. It's a *kaowila*. Now *kaowila* is a tree, but *kaowila* also means something about the spirit of things, about ghosts, and such. The cane originally belonged to the grandfather of Edward Ned Lindsey who was a policeman. His father was sheriff of Lahaina for a long time. It belonged to that family, but it seemed that the family for some reason was not interested in keeping it. They were all a little bit *makau* you know and they didn't want to have it around.

Somehow it made its way to Alice Aki. Now Alice kept it in the attic of her house. It would fall on the ceiling up there and bump around all by itself and she didn't like that. In fact, she was really scared of it. One day she told me, "I have to get rid of this thing. I want to give it to a museum."

"Sure," I said, "we'll get it over there for you." And I forget if I took it over to the museum or if somebody else did (it was a long time ago), but we did. Evidently it is causing no trouble now up in the old Bailey House so I guess it's ok. I think all it wanted to do was to go home where it belonged.

It makes a very nice story.

Lahaina Then

Since the 1930s, I have come out in the public to save historic sites. The Maui Woman's Club, the West Maui Hawaiian Civic Club, the East Maui Hawaiian Civic Club, and the Lauloa Civic Club all took me as an honorary member. I would tell them these things and that's how I came to write my first book.

In Lahaina, Mrs. Alice Kaai was a *hanai* of Kamehameha V of Moloka'i. Her father and grandfather were all governors for him. He gave them the names of children as they were his *hanai*: Kaehukai, the Sea Mist, and Kauialii, the Mysterious Waters. Alice was one of my best friends in Lahaina for over thirty years. She was the one who would go around in my car with me and say,

"Halt! This is such and such a place... This is such and such a *heiau*... This is what happened here." I remember four women in my car at one time telling me these stories and I would write them down. They were the ones helping me with that first book, *Stories of Old Lahaina*.

Then they asked me to write the history of the Catholic Church in the islands and I wrote *Cradle of Faith*. Then I wrote *Mystery of Molokai*. My way was paid to fly to Molokai for a week to write that one.

I had a very beautiful experience in Halawa Valley while I was there, but I never wrote about it. I was out walking by myself and I came to a pool with a stream coming down to a piece of earth like an arrow. There was a great bird there like a *pueo*, an owl, standing on the shaft of earth. When I saw that bird, a name came into my mind: Makuleo. Well, *kuleo* to me is "the cook," yeah? I didn't know what Makuleo meant, but it stayed in my cranium.

I went back to join the rest of the folks I was with. One of them was a Catholic priest and another was the wife of the owner of the Seaside Inn with her little boy. They had all been going their own ways to explore Halawa. I asked them what the name Makuleo meant. They told me that it was where a big *heiau*, Ehupai, had been in Iliopai.

"Who knows about this?" I demanded. "Take me to her?"

So on the way back to the airport, we stopped at a home and the rest stayed in the car while I went on ahead. There was an old lady with beautiful white hair, a lovely Hawaiian woman. I told her who I was and explained that I had been brought to her to ask about the name Makuleo. She told me then of the name and of Iliopai and all of the rest.

Then she said, "My dear, I am so *mehomena,* you see. I have all these things written, but now my leg is hurt and they have burned all my stories or I would give them to you."

Oh, what a loss! All of the legends and happenings of mystery were gone. I have never written anything that she told me that day. I wrote about churches and things like that.

So that was mystical Molokai.

Then I wrote *Kahoolawe*. They offered to pay my way to Honolulu if I would speak to many of the young Hawaiians after the fracas about Kahoolawe and I agreed.

Gosh, how many of them were there that day! I sat down near where the coronation place is, where I used to sit and listen to the Royal Hawaiian Band and I told them of all the things I could think of: what ALOHA means, the wonderful freedom they have, their way of thinking about all of this, how God had helped and protected them by giving them the United States of America to protect them rather than some other country.

Later, one of them came to me down *malihini* at the county building and said, "I was one of the strongest activists in the movement, but since you talked to us, I am no longer an activist. I am going to try to live ALOHA."

When I hear even one thing like that, I feel good. The queen would be pleased; Akukai, Kaiulani...all of them would be pleased. I was thankful that I had lived in the days when you rode a horse around Honolulu. Today all the young people ride around in cars and they never listen. I listened and I learned and now I am able to pass it along. I was glad to be of help because there is so much of beauty to share.

When I was a child growing up, I never went to Lahaina until I was fifteen, yet I knew the people and how they spoke in my time from 1915 to 1920. Always that name was Lahaina and not La-Haina, which means "dead people."

Old Sheriff Saffe said to put this story in my book. He said that the *malihinis* would understand it better if they bought my book so I put it in. It goes like this:

> Once there was a chief from Ka'anapali who was going walking. He was called the Chief of the Red Feet. It was a hot day and he was sweating. As he walked by the haunted pali, he said, "Oh, what a cruel sun and what a hot day! Laha'ina!" L-a-h-a-apostrophe-i-n-a. There's a glottal stop in there. And that's how Lahaina got its name.

The original name was Lele because of all the coming and going in the port. It was a stopping place between the islands for the canoes near the wharf in the old days, especially after the missionaries arrived before they tore the lighthouse down. Lahaiana is another name that was used and it was also known as Malouluokele because of all the ulu trees there. In 1913 they filled in the old Mokuohuiu Pond and Malouluolulu Park. All of this I wrote with the help of the Hawaiian Civic Club.

If you go to Lahaina today, you will see all of the buildings that we were able to save. First we saved the Baldwin House. I used to load cattle with Frank Baldwin. When the union came in about 1939, they wanted to tear the house down and put in a new place like a bowling alley or some darn thing. Well, I couldn't bear for this so I went to Frank and told him that we couldn't let this happen. He spent about $20,000 to restore the house and it's still standing. The Lahaina Restoration Foundation has done a fine job of fixing it up on top of what we did.

There's a funny story about the old Baldwin House. That's where the missionaries lived. The *ali'i* lived up in Wailua. The shipping and market place were down there by Keawehiki Wharf. They used to bring cattle in there and evidently there was a slaughterhouse there also. I think it was Tony Amas, who was one of the hundred men—Mexican cowboys—that came from Mexico to take care of the cattle for Kamehameha III. His house became the Seaman's Hospital and later the old St. Paul

School when the Episcopal nuns were there. The Bridge of Sighs went across the canal from Mokukama Pond into the sea in those days. It was called the Bridge of Sighs because when the sailors came shore, some of them used to walk across it drunk and fall off into the stream. According to the old stories, Amas came in there one day and a steer got loose and chased Dr. Baldwin across the Bridge of Sighs. It must have made a hilarious sight!

It's all changed now. Everything has changed. I wanted to get out of here and leave the islands. Things had changed so that it was just too much for me. I couldn't take it. But where was I to go? I went to visit my son in Mexico, but I couldn't take the climate or the altitude. It was no use going back to Wyoming. I loved San Francisco, but the things I remembered or cared about there were gone, like St. Mary's Church and parts of old Chinatown. During World War II, I worked for the Army Post Office and when I would get very hungry for home food I would go to Chinatown. There was an old Chinese man with a few white hairs in his chin who ran a fine restaurant. When I was tired from working twelve hours a day, seven days a week, I would go there on payday and say, "Do you have any *kung pau* peas or *kai loo*? It's that wine, that Chinese stuff." He said, "You from China?" and I said, "No, Hawaii." After that he became my big friend and I didn't have to worry. When he saw me coming he would get things ready for me.

That was my day. I'm lost in my pasture now, but I still stay. I think maybe it was my destiny to come to Hawaii. This is not in any way a pride. If God wants you to do something in life, you have to learn to listen to your talents and use them to your advantage in order to show Him how much you've done with them afterwards. Something told me that this was what I was here for and I began to write and translate.

I think Queen Liliuokalani would be pleased.

Stories of Rubelite Johnson's Family

Ruby Johnson was an Associate Professor of Indo-Pacific Languages at the University of Hawaii. She has translated the Kumulipo (Hawaiian Creation Chant), which was published by Topgallent Publishing, Honolulu. She shared these family stories on the campus of BYU.

These are stories that are in my family. Some of them I've experienced personally, but others were told to me by my family members.

Uncle Lono and the Blue Lights

Uncle Lono was not living when I was a little girl as this all took place in the 1920s. It seemed that this particular uncle was subject to catatonic fits and every now and then he would simply go stiff and look like a dead person. He married late in life and although he would frequently go into these states of suspension, his wife didn't know this about him. On one of these occasions, she mistakenly assumed that he had died and called the undertaker who promptly arrived and took him away.

They were driving to the mortuary with Uncle Lono in the back when one of the drivers happened to look behind in the *kaa-puka-kahu* (little window) and saw the "body" sitting up. This wasn't as unusual as it might seem, as bodies occasionally do that because of rigor mortis setting in. However, the drivers stopped the hearse and went back to check on their charge. Uncle Lono was very much awake and highly indignant.

"What's the big idea?" he demanded. "Where do you think you're taking me?"

"For goodness sakes!" said the driver. "This man is still alive!"

Needless to say, they turned the hearse around and drove him home. Uncle Lono's wife was amazed to see him. After the drivers had gone and he had offered her an explanation of sorts, she said to him, "You know, it more then surprises me that you go off on these trips of yours. But can you explain one thing? Can you tell me what it is that you do when you're gone like this and why you come back?"

Uncle Lono thought on this for a moment before he slowly replied.

"Well," he said, "I seem to travel around in space. I go all over the universe, I see all of the planets, and then I come home. Other than that, I don't see anything except for these tiny blue lights and I see them all over. They are everywhere."

"What tiny blue lights?" queried his wife. "What do you think they are?"

Uncle Lono was quiet for a moment. Then he spoke. "I suspect I am one of them. I think I am one of these blue lights."

His wife had another question for him. "Can you tell me, on one of these journeys of yours, have you seen a place called Hell? Is it the way the Christians tell about it?"

"I've never seen it," said Uncle Lono, "but I can hear the people crying and moaning and groaning, so let this be a warning to you: don't call anyone to go to a place like that!"

He looked at her and smiled. "You will know when I am really dead and when I'm just off on one of my trips from now on."

And he continued to take his journeys every now and again until the day he really died.

I don't think that we are alone. I think that there is a God and that we go into another life after death. I think there are spirits and if—as Uncle Lono believed as he was floating around out there with all those tiny blue lights—we are indeed spirit, what better thing to be? The whole idea of laying up in store for yourself, a kind of hell behind bars, becomes negative judgment, which I don't think, applies much. In fact I think it may slow you down.

We are each so unique! Other cultures say that our personalities are formed at birth and there is hope for another layer. This may be one reason why we have to be able to handle loneliness. The uniqueness makes you lonely. I don't think any two souls are going to have the same experience at all. We each have to deal with being alone as a self-contained entity and the better we are able to handle this feeling of separation and isolation, perhaps the easier the transition we call "death" will be.

Ekikela Comes Back

This is the story of my great-grandmother, Ekikela (Esther in Hawaiian), who married David Kauiuli. She was a Kaikaula from Moloka'i and she became a Latter Day Saint convert. She gave the Mormon Church the land in East Moloka'i, where the old ward now stands. That is Kaikaula property. She was not really interested in Christianity, but one day she died—and she was gone. Now the old Hawaiians do not believe in burying the body right away, as they have always believed that the spirit can be called back. So they keep the body around for about four days. *(One name for ghosts given by the ancient Hawaiians was wai lua. This particular name described the spirit leaving and the body observed by another person. This wai lua spirit could be driven back into the body by other ghosts or persuaded to come back through offerings or incantations given by living friends so that a dead person could become alive again. It was believed that when life stopped, it was because the spirit had left the body and when life was renewed, it was because the spirit had returned to its former home.)*

They were watching Ekikela's body when, sure enough, sounds began to issue from her throat. Soon she opened her eyes and struggled to sit up. It took her about an hour to recover and for her to speak. Her family began to ask her questions. Where did she go? What did she do? How did she feel?

This is what she told them:

> I was working out in my garden. All I felt was a slight movement of my body upwards. I noticed that I was traveling towards the east and moving automatically without effort towards the sunrise. My journey took me upward until I reached a closed door. The door was slightly ajar, so I looked inside. I saw angels kneeling in prayer. They looked exactly as they had been pictured in the Bible stories I had read. Oh, I thought, what a beautiful place! Maybe I should just try to go in there. I put one foot in the door and out came a hand and knocked me against my chest. I heard a voice say, "Oh no! You are not ready yet. You've got to go back to your body!" He made me turn around and go back to my body then. I didn't really want to and it took me awhile to get back. When I did, my body seemed to be a mountain. I entered through the big toe and began to go up. When I got to the knee, it got dark. When I got to the stomach, it got darker still… and then I woke up!

The Ghost Dog of Poipu

When my parents were courting, they lived in Lawai, Kauai. My mother was Protestant and her father was Reverend Kaili, but my father was Portuguese Catholic. In those days, the garage was built a few hundred feet away from the house. Sometimes my father would drive the car over to the garage to park it for the night as a favor to my grandparents and every time he did, he noticed a white dog, just an ordinary dog, standing around.

Many years later after he had married my mother, my father served as *lua* or head foreman at the stone crusher making

106

gravel to build the Kumooalii Highway, the road that was to join Halfway Bridge to the Lawai gymnasium in Lihue. He would often take us kids riding with him to the construction site where he worked. On this particular morning, he planned to drive the truck to pick up some men and supplies to take them to the site. He had just cranked up the truck and stood up with the tool in his hand when he saw a huge dog sitting on the radiator looking at him with red eyes. He was so afraid that he had simply backed out of the garage all the way up to the house. He came into the kitchen and was speechless for several minutes before he calmed down long enough for him to tell us what happened.

Now it is hard to understand my father's reaction to seeing a dog that had never harmed him unless you are familiar with another story about this animal. Being Catholic, my father didn't eat with us on Fridays but took his dinner with other Catholics in order to have a meatless meal. This Friday he had eaten with his brother and his wife who lived down at New Mill about nine miles to the west of Port Allen. He began to feel a bit sick so he got into the car and started to drive home. In those days, the cars had no doors, just a running board along side. He got sicker and sicker and finally realized he was going blind. He kept driving, but the only thing he could see was a white dog running alongside the car all the way to the house.

Now the place where our house was located near Poipu was called in Hawaiian, The Place of the Dog, and the dog's name is Poki. When my father saw the same dog sitting on the hood of his Deusenburg that morning, he recognized it as the exact dog that had brought him safely home that night. Taking this as a warning, he decided not to go to work that day.

It turned out to be a wise decision for him to stay home as later there was an accident on the construction site. The truck hauling supplies ran off the road and fell into a ravine. Although no one was killed, the truck was demolished and many men were seriously injured. The white dog was a guide and protector for my father. He was the only one who could see it. Nobody else had any contact with the animal—just him.

The last time he saw the dog, it was pawing water near the dam at Wahiawa Gulch on Kauai. Shortly after that, the dam burst, there was a flash flood and several people drowned. My father was safe.

The Three Skulls of Lahaulipua

Back in the 1930s we used to drive down to Lahaulipua just to look across the water. It had been an old Hawaiian battle plain and in those days we found bleaching bones in the sand dunes, remnants from ancient clashes between the chiefs of Oahu and Kauai. If you go there now all you will find is dry rock, dirt, and sand, but when we were kids, there were bones lying about all over the place.

Now my uncle was a Boy Scout leader and when he went away to college, his troupe decided to give him a going-away gift.

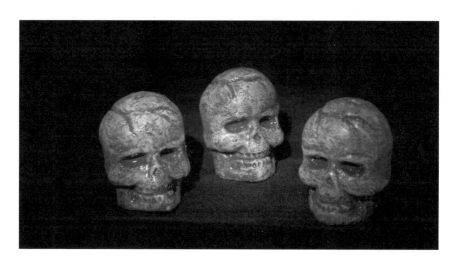

On their last outing to Keoneloa, the boys had found a number of human skulls in perfect condition with full sets of teeth. It was unusual to find skulls with all teeth intact and the scouts proudly presented three of these skulls to my uncle saying, "This is our gift to you. Keep them always."

My uncle thanked them and put the skulls on top of the chiffonier with the glass door in the dining room where we displayed our best china. I remember seeing those skulls all in a row on the top of the cupboard when I was a little kid. When ministers from the church would come to visit, they always asked why those skulls were there.

From the moment my uncle brought those three skulls into the house, there was no peace. Things started to happen. On the first night, unexplained noises and turmoil occurred followed by accidents and arguments. Possessions began to be lost and animals died. Sickness came. Finally life became so bad that my uncle told the skulls:

> "Look! We brought you in out of the hot sun, the wind, and the cold. Why don't you be still? This is a place of protection for you. Won't you stop bringing bad luck to this family?"

After that, it quieted down and nothing more happened concerning the skulls. That is until the day my Aunt Minnie came to visit. She lived a few doors down from us. She told us that from time to time she would drive by our house and see three strange men standing in the road in front of our place. She was curious as to who they might be.

We had no answer for her, but even then we didn't give it much thought. One day, however, Leonard Cavallo, who worked for my father as a stone crusher, said, "You know Kenny, you got some funny people living at your house."

"What people?" said my father.

"There arc thrcc mcn living at your house and they are *funny*!" said Cavallo.

"What do you mean funny?" queried my father.

"Well," Cavallo said slowly, "the other day I saw these three men standing outside your house and I stopped to ask if they'd like a ride to town. They said no thank you, you go ahead and we'll see you there. So I drove on into Koloa. Now it's three miles to town and when I got there I went driving down the main street. When I got to Chang Fook Hee restaurant, *I saw these same three guys sitting in front of the store waiting for me!* They waved at me and when I stopped the car, they said, 'See, we told you we would see you here.' There's no way they could have made it into town before I did because they didn't pass me on the road. You sure do have some funny people living at your house!"

It was a luxury to have an automobile in those days so it was natural for Cavallo to want to share a ride. The main street of town where the Chinese restaurant was located still had hitching posts for the horses to be tied up. It would have been totally impossible for anyone to have beaten Cavallo to town that day. The fact that other people had seen the three men and we never saw them made us wonder. But all our lives we felt that they would look out for us and protect us.

Wahine of the Stone

Our house was located on the edge of a huge gulch and we had taro patches down there. From time to time we would find artifacts. One day my grandmother and I were sitting on the porch when my sister came up to us carrying three stones she had found in the gulch. One was a large stone that had obviously been worked by human hands. The other two were pieces that looked like adze blades, one of which was nicely polished. My grandmother suggested that she put them on the large stone pillars that extended up to the veranda. We both watched her place the large rock down first with the two smaller pieces on top.

That night my grandmother stayed up late after the rest of the family had gone to bed. She heard a loud noise outside on the porch, but when she checked, no one was there. She went to bed, fell asleep, and had a vivid dream. She was hanging laundry on a clothesline strung over the gulch when she saw a Hawaiian man in a red *malo.* He spoke to her and said, "Don't you know I gave those stones to the water?"

The next morning she walked out to the porch to look for the stones. They were gone. She found them in the flower garden about twenty feet away where they had been thrown during the night. No one in the family had been near them. She picked them up and brought them into our house to sit among the other *pohaku* (sacred stones) that we kept.

One of these stones we called "the Woman of Ni'ihau." She belongs to the island of Ni'ihau although my Aunt Mary found her in a yard on Oahu. When Aunt Mary died in the 1930s, my grandmother brought her things home from Oahu and this particular stone that my aunt had salvaged was placed on a table facing the front of our house.

At this time in our lives, my father ran a fishing business, a *hukilau*, and we would market our fish from Hunilau to Kapaa. When we had a catch, we would go out to the islands at Hanaho and split it with the folks who came down to the beach to help us haul in the nets. After the fish had been distributed, we took what was left to market. One of the things we did was open up the fishing grounds in the old Hawaiian way by taking a fish and facing the head to the sea (this is called the *ki*) to honor the tradition of always giving the first fish caught back to the sea for the purpose of securing abundance later.

When we went there, we lived with an old man named Ho'ohana. It was said that Ho'ohana knew *ana'ana'* or sorcery. He had struck his wife once and she was blind in one eye that would often weep. Their house was sparsely furnished and divided by two doors, one facing north and one facing south. One night my brother and I were lying on Ho'omana's bed. I was awake and I saw the shadow of a head moving very slowly across the wall. As it crossed the window, the shadow was cast on the tree outside. I was petrified and heard my brother call out for our mother, but we didn't tell about it then. It wasn't until years later when both of us were in our late forties that we visited up in Kamuela and I asked if he remembered that night.

"Did you see what I saw?" I asked. "I saw a shadow of a head move across the wall, splash on the tree trunk outside, and stop."

"That's not what I saw," he said. "I saw a real head that had been decapitated moving across the wall!"

One day after our fishing operations, my father brought Ho'omana and his wife to our house. The first time he stepped in, he walked over and sat down not far from the Ni'ihau Stone, the lady of the sea, which rests in the southern opening of the house. I clearly remember that my brother was with the old man in the dining room where the three skulls were kept, my mother was in the kitchen frying chicken, and I was in the back bedroom. All of a sudden I heard a commotion. When I ran into the dining room, I saw the old man down on his hands and knees crawling toward the Ni'ihau Stone. When he reached it, he started praying and begging for forgiveness. We finally calmed him and got him to a chair. My brother said that he had heard a slap and had seen the old man thrown off his chair. It had sounded like a woman's slap. The old man agreed. Yes it was true. It was a woman's hand that had slapped him hard and knocked him off the chair. He declared that there was "something" in the house and he sensed it came from the Ni'ihau Stone. The stone was a *puula*, a fish stone, and held a place of importance in our family. It often figured in my mother's dreams and my father would dream of the stone as a woman wearing a bandanna on her head who would often tell him where to fish.

One of the things we did was garland the stone with *maunaloa leis*. Every day my mother would go to the *maunaloa* vine to pick blossoms to weave into *leis*. We knew she was supposed to have Ni'ihau shell leis as the stone was from that island, but we didn't have the shells so we substituted Maunaloa instead. Now and then, when we were at the beach, we would smell *Maunaloa* on the trade winds coming from the sea. There was no *Maunaloa* there of course and we knew it was the stone.

The stone played a part in our lives all during the time I was growing up. When I was fifteen, I was vice president of the Missionary Youth Fellowship. We had been studying the Ten Commandments at our Friday night youth meetings and to sum up the study we decided to join the three churches to present a skit that I had been chosen to write. On the night before the rehearsal I sat in the parlor with the Ni'ihau stone to write the story of the Ten Commandments from the Bible. I went through Genesis, Exodus, and Levidicus in order to get the whole story. I was busily assigning parts to the players like Aaron and Moses. The part of God was assigned to a voice off stage. I had gotten the script going and working well when suddenly the entire set of papers was thrown onto the floor as if by an invisible hand. It was late at night and there was no wind at all. I picked up the papers and returned them to the table, and then decided not to continue.

Early the next morning, I put the finishing touches on the manuscript and went to church. All of the kids were there along with the minister, the superintendent, and his aides. As they went through my script, they began to disagree with the way it was written saying that I had mistaken the biblical story. I replied that while it was not the story I had been taught in Sunday school, it was the story that had been written in the Bible. I turned to the biblical passages that demonstrated how the commandments had been written first by the hand of God himself and the second time, he had Moses do it. It stated clearly that the people knew the commandments before Moses went up the mountain to receive them. The group could not agree with this, however, and they decided to rewrite the script and reschedule the play. This they did.

After I went home that night, I couldn't sleep. My grandmother and I were sitting in the kitchen discussing the incident when we clearly heard a woman's voice speak from the parlor. It was as plain as day. I had a cup of cocoa in one hand and a cracker in the other and I said to my grandmother, "Did you hear anything?"

"Yes, I did."

"What did you hear?"

"A woman's voice."

"Where did it come from?" I wanted to be sure.

"From the parlor."

We both got up and went into the parlor thinking that perhaps somebody had come in from the street. There was no one there. I still believe it was the voice of the woman of the stone who had taken an interest in my spiritual education.

Rachel Moki and the Black Pig

In the old days on Kauai, Paloa Plantation belonged to the Rice family. In order to geographically join the plantation, a tunnel was cut through the mountain range that ran between two sections of the land. The name of the mountain was Hoary Head Range where Queen Victoria's Head is located. I was in high school when the Filipinos from Banana Camp, who had been building the tunnel, refused to go to work. After they had been digging and blasting on the project for some time, they reported seeing a giant come into the tunnel and point away from the path they were building. After three of the men died in accidents, the rest refused to go back to work. In order to solve the problem of the shutdown, Grove Farm and Kapuna Plantation hired a *kahuna*, Rachel Moki.

We called her the "bearded lady" because she actually had a beard. She met with the Goat Farm Plantation officials at Lake Waika and asked them to bring a sacrificial pig. The pig was brought. She then announced that in order to bring the men back to work to complete the tunnel, it was necessary to sacrifice the black pig. If the pig made no noise when led into the water, if it did not squeal but simply went down, then the sacrifice would be accepted. If the pig squealed and made a lot of noise, all would know that the sacrifice was not acceptable.

We all watched closely as the pig was led into the water of the lake. It was a little pig and it went under the water without a sound. Now you show me a pig that doesn't squeal when put into water! Any animal will fight for its life, but this little pig just accepted its fate.

The men returned to work and the tunnel was completed. Of course some people will tell you that it was all a psychological ploy to get the men back to work, but that doesn't explain why the pig didn't squeal.

I can see through relating these experiences that there are signs and warnings that come to you throughout your lifetime. They do have meaning. We must recognize them and listen to them when they appear.

Auntie Harriet Ne of Molokai

Auntie Harriet Ne of Molokai was known throughout the Hawaiian Islands as a master storyteller and respected font of Hawaiian ways and culture. This interview was conducted at Kaunakakai, Molokai, in 1983.

A Tale of Night Marchers

It was in October of 1958. I was visiting one of my friends, a teacher at the school here on Molokai. One night she went to work late in her classroom. She didn't want to go alone, so I told her I would go with her. Her house was right across from the school so we walked up to her room. She was busy doing her bookwork when we heard the voices

"Auntie Harriet," she said, "what is that?"

"Oh," I replied, "it's only somebody chanting."

"I'm getting goose bumps!" she cried.

"Come over here and sit down," I suggested, "or better yet, let's go outside and watch. I think it might be the Night Marchers going fishing."

"No, I don't want to look!" she said, but then she changed her mind. "Oh yes, I want to look. I *want* to see what they look like!"

We went over to stand by the classroom door when I remembered my childhood warnings.

"They mustn't see us. They will vanish if they do and some say it's dangerous."

She looked at me and we sat down on the floor. We heard the chanting coming closer and closer. Then we saw them. There were about twenty. I counted. The first to come was a tall man—I think he was one of the chiefly class—and his legs were brown and so husky. I tried to look at their faces, but I couldn't see a face. All I could see was from the chest down.

"What is it?" whispered my friend.

"Those are Night Marchers all right," I told her. My friend was Italian and from the old country, but her husband was a local boy.

"I heard about them before, but I never believed it," she said softly. "My husband told me, but I didn't believe him. Now I can say that I really saw them. Now I believe in Night Marchers! Where are they going?"

"They're going straight down to the beach. There's a pathway," I said in a low voice. "They're going right through Kapuni's kitchen too because Kapuni built that house right in the path of the Marchers."

Sure enough, they walked right down into the house belonging to Kapuni and disappeared!

Years after that, my aunt bought Kapuni's house and we used to go and spend weekends there. One night I told her, "You know Auntie Hattie, I want to come up here in October and sleep over."

"Do you want to celebrate your birthday with me?" she said.

"Yes, that too," I smiled, "but I also want to see the Night Marchers."

"Oh yeah," she replied, "they come right through our house. You don't have to go outside. Our kitchen is right in the pathway of the Night Marchers."

That October, my mother and father and all us kids went up to stay with my Aunt Hattie. Now my auntie had one unusual *calabash* on top of her screened-in pie safe where she kept her food. The *calabash* was filled with eggs that night and all of a sudden it began to rock. The eggs were rattling like crazy.

"What's that?" I cried.

"It's the Night Marchers coming," said Auntie Hattie calmly. "See, the *calabash* is making noise. Come. Come look at it."

I tiptoed over and peeked in.

"Uh oh," I said, "the eggs' going to break. Better I take them out."

"So far," said Auntie, "for five years never had one broken egg."

Then we heard the chanting.

"Oh, they're coming! They're closer now!"

I ran down the hallway into the living room and looked out the window. I saw all of these torches coming down the mountain in a straight line. The chanting seemed to come from the back of the line. The leaders just walked straight ahead without looking to the right or the left. The chief was leading. The high priest and what appeared to be a lesser chief followed him. The fishermen must have been in the back because those were the ones carrying the nets. There were some women in the line too, but I saw mostly men. They were going fishing, marching down to the sea to go fishing.

I heard my little brother say, "Want to sleep over there."

"No, no!" cried my aunt. "That's where they gonna walk."

My brother was always the stubborn one. "I like to see if they gonna walk on me," he grinned.

"You better not sleep over there or they gonna walk on you and you gonna have every bone broken in your body!" said Auntie.

"Aaaaah, I don't believe it," he sneered and he went over and plopped down on the couch right by the front door. My auntie ran over and yanked him off the sofa just as we saw them march in the front door. They both crouched down on the floor as the Night Marchers came through the room. They filed right down the hallway into the kitchen and right out the back of the house. My brother was such a rascal, even if he sees, he don't believe. He reached out his hand and tried to catch one of the legs of a fisherman, but the guy just lifted up his feet and kept on walking!

The Missing Girl and the Mu People

It was in 1924 that Ella was kidnapped by the old Filipino man. She was my high school classmate and she was only fifteen years old. He was in his late sixties when he asked her to marry him. Of course, she didn't want to so he kidnapped her and took her way out in the country on the way to his house. Knowing the police would come after them, he veered off on the trail that led to the caves by the sea. When he saw some old clothes and canvas lying around the caves, he decided they would make a good hideout.

On Molokai there is what is called a "Spring Triangle," three springs of fresh water located in the shape of a triangle. The old man knew where one of these springs was located so he got water from there and took fish from the sea. That is how they lived.

Ella's parents were so upset! Now Ella was my dear friend and we were all upset so we got together with the Boy Scouts and the Girl Scouts and we combed the island to look for her. Although we didn't know where to begin, we knew the old man was interested in her and we thought of a place he might have taken her. We had each child line up ten feet apart with a stick to poke around to search for her. We walked all the way up the island. Sheriff Lindsey was with us and when we came to a place where the trail went off to the cliffs, he said, "Let's go on the main road and branch off. Let the police go down to look."

"Can I go with the police?" I asked.

"Sure," he said, "if they're willing to take you."

I asked Old Charlie if I could go with them and he said, "Okay, you come with me."

I went with him and we came to a path that was so slippery with smooth dirt that we had to hang onto vines and stones that stuck out of the cliff in order to make our way along. There were parts of the trail where there was nothing to hang onto so I dug my fingers into the earth and soon my nails were all chipped and bleeding. But I hung on and hoped that I wouldn't slide down off of the cliff.

When Charlie reached the cave, he grabbed my hand and pulled me up.

"You go in because you are small," he said. "You can crouch through that *puka* (hole)."

He had a flashlight and he shone the beam into the cave after I had crawled in.

"What do you see in there?" he said.

"Some old clothes and a blanket, some fish bones and some *opii* shells," I replied. "Looks like somebody living here."

"Do you think it's the girl?" said Charlie.

"No, I don't think so." Then I asked if I could come out because the air in the cave was foul and I was getting a headache. The smell in that cave was terrible.

Charlie told me to walk over to a place where I could breathe fresh air from the ocean. As I walked, I noticed a sash lying on the ground and I knew it was Ella's. We had dresses made the same. Her dress was red and white while mine was green and white.

"Charlie!" I called out. "This is Ella's sash. She must be around here somewhere!"

Charlie told me to wait there until the rest of the policemen came. When they caught up with us, we told them what we had found in the cave. They asked me if I would go back in there with them. Three of the policemen—the skinny ones—squeezed in with me. At the side of the cave, we found the fish bones and a bottle of drinking water. Then I got really curious when I noticed what appeared to be a pathway leading further into the cave. It was so dark I asked one of the policemen if I could have a flashlight. When he asked me why I wanted it, I told him that I wanted to go further back into the cave. He agreed to go with me and we walked into the darkness together.

That is when we saw them. The policeman suddenly flashed his light against the cave wall and there were all of these half-clothed people with their backs up against the stone. They wore just a cloth wrapped around their bodies to cover them. Their hair was long and thick and they had muscles. I especially noticed the muscles in their arms and legs. They had bushy eyebrows, but the strangest thing of all was their smooth faces: no beards, no mustaches, no nothing. Their faces were smooth, but at the same time all wrinkled and brown like old leather. There were maybe six of them and they all seemed to be afraid. I don't think they were so much afraid of us, but of the beam from the flashlight. When we saw they were afraid, we just backed out without saying a word and left them alone.

After we got outside, I asked the policeman, "Who was that? What kind of people are they?"

"I think they are the Mu," he said, "the last tribe of Mu. They were here before the Menehune and before the Hawaiians came to the islands."

"I've never heard of them," I said. "I've heard of the last tribe of Menehune, but not of Mu."

"Not many people have ever seen them except some of the ranch hands," said the policeman. "Sam Barras said he saw footprints of the Mu in the sand where they went fishing, I guess. He said that the footprints were regular-sized, but very wide and flat. The Hawaiians who live around here tell of the Mu people in one of their chants though, so they must have known about them."

I remember not feeling afraid at all when I saw them although I was surprised to find people there in the cave. Later I learned of a principal at one of the schools who wanted to do research on this tribe, the last tribe of Mu people, as he called them. He was very interested in the project, but he moved to Oahu and died in Wahiawa. I don't think he completed his work."

Ella was found three months later. It was her little dog that took the sheriff to her. They located her down in a gully not far from the caves we had explored. She was on one side of the ravine in a small place where two boulders came together to form a shelter. She had been brutally assaulted. She was not herself after that.

The police took the old Filipino man to jail on Maui after they found him still working in the pineapple fields.

And that was how I came to see the last of the Mu people.

I Meet the Menehune

The year I saw the Menehune was the same year I went to Niihau. It was 1938. There is a long ledge in the Wet and Dry Caves on Kaui and that is where they like to live. I went there with two of my friends. We knew that Menehunes eat guava and fish so we picked guavas. They were so sweet. I never ate so many guavas in my life! Then we hid behind a tree and my friend told me to be quiet.

"If you make noise," he said, "they won't come. They are all down at the beach fishing."

We waited behind the tree and pretty soon we heard guttural noises. They make such funny noises. I guess they were talking among themselves.

"Look!" said my friend. "You can just see their heads."

I looked and all I could see was the back of their heads. They were fishing, but then they came ashore and we got a good sight. We could almost see them face-to-face. They were short, not big but husky. They were not brown and that surprised me for some reason. They were kind of fair and many were very fair. There were both men and women. The women had long hair and the men had long barbs, which they had twisted into a pug and put a stick through. The men also had smooth faces. I don't think they shaved with a sharp shell or anything. I think they must not have had hair on their faces because of their body chemistry. Some of the men were wearing old cut trousers. One lady had on an old white tee shirt and a pair of bright red suspenders. That's what attracted me—her suspenders!

I saw the Menehune again in 1948 on the Big Island. I was visiting a friend, Mrs. Johanson, at Puna. She is German-Hawaiian and she keeps all of the old Hawaiian customs. She prepared our dinner and served dried fish and *poi.* Just as we were about to sit down to eat, she said, "Let's take our plates out on the *lanai* and eat there."

"Why?" I asked.

"Oh," she replied, "I like to look at the ocean when I eat. I really enjoy that and besides I'm expecting some friends."

So I said okay and we took our dishes outside. She had an old-fashioned walnut table and chairs out there so we sat down and began to eat. All of a sudden, the dogs started to bark and charged for the gate. Mrs. Johanson yelled at the dogs to come back and said that her friends were coming.

When I looked up, I thought they were children and said, "Oh, the neighbor's children?"

"Oh no," she smiled. "Just wait."

Her guests came up to the *lanai* and made funny guttural noises down in their throats. I think they were saying *aloha* to her. There were two of them and evidently there were usually three as she asked where the other one was and they made motions that he was sleeping. Mrs. Johanson made a motion in return for them to come, sit down, and eat. They then went under the table and put their hands out with their palms up. She put the fish in their hands and then got a *calabash* of *poi* and put it under the table for them. They continued to sit there under the table and didn't come up at all.

"What kind of game is this?" I said. "What kind of people are they?"

"Hawaiian," said Mrs. Johanson.

"They don't look like Hawaiians," I said.

"Oh, but they are," she replied. "They are Menehune. You know the Menehune?"

"Yeah, the short people, the small people, the midgets of the Hawaiian race," I said. "But they're not Hawaiian, hah?"

"Oh yes, they are Hawaiians," she replied. "They must be. They were here before the Hawaiians even landed. They are my friends."

She went on to tell me that whenever she works down in her *taro* patch, she tells the Menehune exactly what she wants done and the next day everything is done exactly so. In one of her *taro* patches, she said, is a spring of fresh water that opens out into the ocean. Whenever she is hungry for a special fish that she loves to eat she sends a Menehune down into the water to catch one for her.

"Do you know what I heard about the Menehune?" I said. "I heard that they don't care for the water and they don't want to go in above their waist. They are scared of the water."

But Mrs. Johanson denied this.

"Oh no! This one dives into the spring and swims out to the ocean and catches my fish for me. You don't believe me? You wait. I'll tell him to go."

She spoke Hawaiian to the little people and they seemed to understand. One thing I noticed. When she spoke to them, their eyes lit up and their eyebrows went up as if they were puzzled. Then she repeated what she had said and their eyes twinkled.

They muttered, "Heh, heh, heh, heh." And off they raced to the sea.

And that's what happened that day.

124

The Great Storyteller Richard Marks & Friends

The following conversation took place in the tiny library at Kalaupapa Leper Colony on the Island of Molokai three days before Christmas 1983. The sound of singing drifted in the window from the chapel across the street providing a contrasting mood to the topics we were discussing. Richard Marks, sheriff of Kalaupapa and local historian, Kuulei Bell, the librarian, and residents of the colony who did not wish to give their names were present. It was a memorable visit.

Kalaupapa Talk Story

"Talk about Chokeneck!" exclaimed Richard Marks. "It happened to me one night at home in bed. I had retired for the night and planned on reading myself to sleep. I had picked up a book on *huna* and had just opened the first page. I hadn't read a word when I became so drowsy that I just put it aside and fell asleep. I woke up suddenly with something pushing me down into the bed. My eyes were open and I tried to holler for my wife who was sleeping in the same room, but nothing would come out. Then I remembered that I had once heard to make a prayer or the sign of the cross for protection. I couldn't move any part of me. I was totally paralyzed and this thing was pushing me down. Finally I was able to make the sign of the cross with my little finger and bang! The thing disappeared. I hollered then! As soon as the pressure was off, boy did I make a noise! My wife almost fell out of bed. She later gave me hell for reading a book on *huna* just before I went to sleep thinking that might have caused it, but I did not read the book. I just opened the first page. A few days later, I did read the book and it said that the phenomenon of "Chokeneck" is one of the ways a *kahuna* can get you. I don't know what the connection is. I only know it happened."

"I didn't say anything to my two daughters," he continued. "They didn't know anything about it, but it happened to them next. First to Eloise, the youngest, and then to Rita when she went to sleep. In fact, it woke her up. They were so upset, they took their sleeping mats and went into my wife's bed, but then decided they didn't want to wake her up so they came into my room and woke me up instead. I had to go into their bedroom and put Hawaiian salt all over the place. *Ti* leaves are supposed to be good too."

"My auntie practiced *kahuna-ism*," said Kuulei Bell. "My mother's oldest sister, but she is the only one I know. She doesn't do it anymore. She gave it up. She's old now. My mom used to tell us about it. I said I don't believe in it, but she'd say, 'no dear, I'm telling you the truth.' My auntie changed completely, but she continued to practice. It is said that if you do that very long, you cannot have one normal child. She had twelve children and all

Richard Marks, a survivor of Hansen's Disease, is sheriff of Kalupapa, Molokai. The former Leper Colony was named a National Historical Park in 1980. A handful of patients have chosen to remain. All are now cured. *Courtesy of the Associated Press.*

Paul Harada, a resident of Kalaupapa, was a survivor of Hansen's Disease.
Courtesy of the Associated Press.

her kids got something wrong. Her husband's father was one big *kahuna*, the kind who would throw a curse and then send a spirit out."

"Oh yeah, *ana'ana*," Richard broke in, "the black magic, the evil arts. Most forms of *huna* are good, like the healing arts, but like anything else, a darker side developed white magic and black magic. There's always somebody who's going to corrupt it when they get that kind of power. Like fire, it's all in how you use it."

"The *kahuna* was a technical man," he continued, "a medicine man and a priest. The top warriors, navigators, and genealogists

127

were all *kahunas*. Different branches, that's all. But these were the best brains they had. These people were the ones who kept the knowledge and passed it down from generation to generation. Sad thing, huh, when they wanted to pass it down and their own family wasn't interested. Then it's better if some outsider comes in and learns it rather than having them die and take the knowledge with them. In Hawaii, each village had their own genealogist and each kept their own records. People from Upper Molokai never knew that much about Kalaupapa Village, so if a line died out in Kalaupapa, the people in Upper Molokai knew just a little but they didn't have the full background. Iolani Luahine's father kept to the strings. He knew the genealogies for twenty-six generations back. The old man showed me the stuff. I said, give it to the kids and pass it down. Ah, he said, they only make fun. These young Hawaiians, they're not doing it on purpose. They just like to tease. That kind of stuff…when it's lost, it's lost."

"Kalaupapa. The patients who came were a completely different kind of society from the original Hawaiian village. The Leprosy patients came from all over. They didn't have anybody from generation to generation keeping the knowledge of the families alive. As sheriff, I get all kinds of calls from people trying to trace their family records. I try to help them, but most of the time I can't find out. They used to give babies born in Kalaupapa false birth certificates so they wouldn't know where they came from. I got a call just last week from a man who is in his sixties. His grandmother raised him and didn't want the stigma of coming from the Leper Colony placed upon him, so she never told him that he was born here. Just before she died, she told her oldest son. I said why did you wait so long? He replied that his uncle had told him just before *he* had died. It's so sad and I feel helpless, but with the records this way it can't be helped. I asked David Kapele, but he cannot remember. May Sing was the best. She remembered a lot of people. You've got the same knowledge outside, but it's different. Outside people live regular lives, they have families (there are no children in Kalaupapa), they are busy and they see things changing. Here the knowledge is concentrated. So many of the people were blind from the disease for fifty or sixty years. I used to love to talk to the old folks. They have so much to offer. They sat around for years and they kept the stories alive. It was a mark of respect. Today we have our minds cluttered with everything else, television, books, whatever."

"Oh, but we used to have the *kahunas* around here!" Kuulei exclaimed. "There was one who lived on the other side of the river when we first came in the forties. He was an old man then, the old man Nailima, and he used to catch fireballs in his hand. *Aulele.* Yeah, really! Jack and Mary Sing, the Mormon Bishop and his wife, told me this. Somebody sends the fireball and somebody else gonna get sick from it, so old man Nailima would intercept it and catch it in his hand. The blood would actually come out of the thing. All blood in his hand, you know. But you must be strong to do that. He would actually catch'um in his hand and oh the blood!"

"Fireballs!" Richard said. "I saw one on Maui once that had a color like fire. I was sitting in front of my auntie's house talking to my brother Eddie when I was just a young kid. We were doing our favorite thing, reading the comics, and Auntie is talking to her neighbor over by the fence. All of a sudden, I looked up and I saw the two old ladies blessing themselves and staring at the road in front of the house. I saw this thing about three and a half feet up off the ground like it's floating straight down the road by the fence. I was paralyzed and couldn't take my eyes off it. My auntie was praying like crazy she was so scared. We watched it go straight down the road to the rock crusher and when it reached there it went straight up to the top. The guy who ran the rock crusher was an old Korean man. He was a real nice guy until he got drunk and then he had a real mouth on him. There had been a big *luau* that Saturday night and my uncle had gone to it. He said the guy had gotten into an argument with an old Hawaiian man. They warned him. They told him to watch out, that the old Hawaiian man was a *kahuna,* but he said, 'baloney. I don't believe that kind of rubbish.' The old Hawaiian man said, 'shut up boy, you don't fool around with me,' and he had replied, 'nonsense!' When that fireball got to the rock crusher, the Korean man had a heart attack. When they got him to the hospital, he was dead. Some said it was sent after him. Others maintained that it was just lightning and coincidence. I have seen lightning and St. Elmo's Fire in Alaska and this fireball was a completely different thing."

"So many things happen," Kuulei mused. "My mom used to say when I'd come home from school, I would have this big white dog who used to follow me. *Aumakua,* you know, a god to protect. The dog would be tiny when we'd start out and as we'd walk, he would grow. By the time we got to the house, he would be as big as me. The dog would stay outside of the gate and I would walk in the house. My brother Ruben would see him too. When I used to come, the dog would wait outside. But I never see that stuff. My mom is Hawaiian and she told me not to be afraid because I was *kapu.* She told me I would never see spooks because I had protection. I never saw the dog, but others did."

"The white dog is very special to the Hawaiians," Richard mused.

The art teacher wanted to ask a question. "Do you ever have Menehunes around here?"

The librarian spoke up. "Yes, you can go to Kona for them."

"I just wondered," said the teacher, "because a friend of mine said she saw one in a pool on Maui. Dead."

"Dead?" repeated the librarian.

"A dead Menehune?" said Richard.

"Yeah," replied the teacher. "It was floating in a pool. It looked like it was about the size of a baby and it was covered with white hair like a beard and hair all over its body. It scared them and they ran back and told some other people. They were just wandering around up by Seven Sacred Pools and they both saw it floating in the water. They thought it was a baby at first. Scared them good."

"Well, that would be the place if they were on Maui," said Richard. "I've only heard of them in Iao Valley, but I've never seen them myself. When the 1946 tidal wave wrecked the breakwater in Lihue, they went there and built a new breakwater. They put it in one way and every time they went out to work, they would see fresh footprints. And they kept doing that and finally they turned the breakwater around the other side and the footprints disappeared. Like somebody was trying to tell them not to build it that way. The Menehunes were rock builders famous for stonewalls. They were the greatest stonemasons in the Pacific. Some refer to them as the "first Hawaiians" before the Hawaiians even landed. The Menehune Fishpond on Kaui is attributed to them and the Menehune Ditch. Then they disappeared. What happened to them? Maybe like what happened to the pixies in England. They had a lot of forests and little people there at first, but as the bigger people came in, they would either enslave or kill them. Perhaps that's why the Menehunes retreated up into the mountains. Maybe that's why they only come out at night.

"I don't believe they were only six inches tall, but perhaps they were small like pygmies."

"Yeah, these islands are special all right. So many things here are unique. I remember when Iolani Luahine used to come. We got to be very good friends. I took her up in the old crater once. She wanted to go there and I was her guide. I'll never forget it. There was no wind at all that day or the slightest breeze. We walked down into the crater and she started to chant, all in Hawaiian of course. She chanted and she chanted and it got stronger and stronger. All of a sudden, her hair began to stand straight up all over her head, just like she had stuck her finger in an electrical socket! I was the only one to see."

"She was a wonderful old lady. She was a great one and so full of stories. She said that she was born to be a *kahuna.* Her mother had been told the future before Iolani was even born. She was not supposed to marry, as she would lose *mana* if she did. She went ahead and got married anyway and she did suffer from a lot of hard luck after that. It seems if you go too deeply into *huna* that you can easily become unbalanced and she knew this. After a point, she began to concentrate on *hula* instead. I always thought she was much older than she was. There was something timeless about her. I went to her wake. I was talking to Reverend Akaka and he was telling me how she used to be a real clown and what a wonderful spirit she was right up until the very end. When he went to see her in the hospital, she would walk down the hall teasing him as she dragged her bottle of intravenous liquid. Nothing stopped her. A beautiful lady. Oh, she was good. Just before she died, the state of Hawaii finally did something decent. They made her a State Historical Figure. I wish they would do more of that for these old people who give so much to the rest of us."

"Oh yes, this is a special place with special people. You look at a map of Kalaupapa and right in the center you got a little piece of land sticking out this side of Wainao Valley. That was where the *ana'ana* held their sacred rites, gathering every five or six years. This is where the marriages were set up in all Hawaii. We had so many *heiaus* here, more than any place else in Hawaii. Dozens of family shrines, the large Dog Heiau, sweet potato planting patch walls on the other side. I got into a big argument with Bishop Museum about that. They told me no such thing. I talked to Iolani Luahine and she heard of it when she was a child. There was an old man who used to travel with her, little good-looking old cowboy, and he had seen the same thing on the Big Island when he was little. He said they planted it with sweet potatoes inside the stone walls."

"Plus we had the longest sled run in the Hawaiian Islands right here. The contractors bulldozed the whole thing. It was all built up with grass all over it and the ancient Hawaiians would wet it down, run with their sleds just like toboggans and jump on it. It's hard to imagine if you've never seen one. Now Christmas Berry has taken over and it's all lost. I guess it would have taken too many permits and clearances from the Health Department to bring archaeological crews over here to do extensive work and they just didn't bother. Oh, I've gotten into so many arguments over all this. I used to get into so much *huhu* (trouble). Like my father told me: the squeaky wheel gets the grease, but the empty drum makes the most noise; hollow-head, the emptier it is, the more noise it makes!"

"Ah well, I've been 'official gadfly' for so many years, I'm beginning to mellow out a bit. Things change and some things even for the better. Other things are lost and it can't be helped or stopped. Most of it is good."

There was a short silence as the conversation lapsed. The strains of recorded Christmas carols could be clearly heard from the little church across the road. Kuulei stood to leave and the rest of us followed suit.

Richard looked up and smiled.

"Aw, what the heck," he said. "Merry Christmas!"

Ghost Lover

Kuulei Bell was a resident of the settlement at Kalaupapa on Moloka'i for many years. She suffered from Hansen's disease.

You know what once happened? I never told this to anybody except my husband. We have lived in Kalaupapa for years and I have a very warm and comfortable home, you know. The house has been blessed and we have been very happy living there. Well, my husband is always cold and I'm always hot so he cannot sleep against me or I kick him off. I usually lie down with him and as soon as he sleeps, I take off. This particular night, I went into the front room to sleep and a funny thing happened to me. The strangest thing! I felt someone else get into bed with me! This individual was warm; he was holding me and he wanted to make love to me. I was not afraid. I could actually feel him holding me and I knew that he wanted me. I could feel the warmth of his body and solidarity of him. I was just going to sleep when this happened, and I said to myself, 'what is this?' I could sense his wanting me. Now who do I know that would love me that much to come back to make love to me, heh? My mom? Nah, this was definitely not my mom, this was a man!

I got up and went in the back room to wake my husband up and tell him what had happened. When I told him what I'd experienced, he asked if I hadn't been dreaming. I told him it was no dream! I knew what I had felt. I told my husband that night, but I never told anyone else. Who you going to tell? You going to tell your mother that there's this invisible guy who climbed into bed and tried to make love to me and gave me a good scare? Who you going to tell? It was funny that I wasn't afraid though. And it never happened again.

It began to make more sense a few weeks later when the same thing happened to my friend Rachel. There she was telling me the same thing and I just listened to what she had to say and didn't tell her I had the same experience. I didn't say a word. She lived just a few houses away from me. One night, she said, a man crawled in bed with her and tried to make love to her when she was sleeping. When she turned on the lights to investigate, there was nobody there. She swore it wasn't a dream and that it really happened. She said that she could feel the warmth of this individual and that she was not afraid. It was exactly the same that had happened to me, and yet I didn't tell her that she wasn't alone in this. I don't know why. I just couldn't say anything about it.

I wonder who it was?

The Legend of the L'iang L'iang Tree

Richard Marks is a master storyteller. He shared this amazing story as he drove us along the bumpy road from Kalaupapa to Kalawao to visit Father Damien's chapel. We jounced along in his old station wagon hitting every rut and bump in the road as he pointed out the sites of this chilling personal experience.

Well, I can only relate what happened to me when I was young, and that was a long time ago. My dad and my uncle had gone to Kalawao for the day. They were usually home before dark, but this day they didn't show up and my mom was worried so she sent me to see what had happened to them. I started off in this old Model-T Ford that I had and found them up here past Damien's chapel at the end of the point. They were fine. They had been talking story and had just forgotten about the time so they went home and I followed in that old car. I had gotten into the habit of saving gasoline back then as gas was expensive and we didn't have much money, so I would cut the motor at the top of the hill and coast to the bottom as far as I could go. It was just past dusk and there was this full moon so bright that you could cast a shadow. It was almost like day.

It was just about here that I had come so you can see what a steep hill this really is. I was just passing Damien's water tank and true to form, I cut the motor and proceeded to coast down the hill. I had just hit the crest of the hill when all of the dogs started acting funny. I had four of them with me and they were with me most of the time. We call them our "kids" in the settlement as children were never allowed in Kalaupapa because of the leprosy. If a baby was born here, it was immediately taken away from its mother and to another island to raise, so our dogs were the only "kids" we had. We had been through a lot together, but this night for some strange reason all of them started to growl and their hair was standing straight up on end. There was nothing around that I could see, but as we silently coasted towards the bottom of they hill they got more and more agitated and—strangest of all—started snapping at the thin air with their teeth. Geez, I tell you, it made the hair stand up on the back of my neck. It was really quiet with no wind at all except the breeze from the motion of the car as we coasted along.

Just as we hit the bottom of the hill and the dogs were really upset, I saw *it*. I can't explain what *it* was, I only know I saw this thing standing right there under the L'iang L'iang tree to the left of the road. *It* was grey and shiny, about five feet tall and as real and solid as you or I. *It* just stood there and the dogs went wild as we coasted past. I couldn't turn my head to look, but I saw *it* as we slipped by. I was so scared that I drove all the way home in second gear and didn't stop to shift once. I jammed into the garage and my uncle came out to see what was the matter.

"Oh, nothing," I said, trying to appear cool.

"Don't tell me nothing!" snapped my uncle. "I'm blind, not deaf. Why did you come racing into the garage in second gear?"

So I told him what had happened and then he understood. There is a legend about that place and we all knew it very well. Of course the stories vary, but it seems that in the original settlement during the lawless times, it really was the survival of the strongest. The strong ones were the ones who lived. All of this country was bare then with no foliage at all. This Christmas Berry came just recently after the state bulldozed the land and then left it. In the old times, it was just desolate rocky land with little shacks, not even houses, and rare was the one with a window, dotting all of this ground.

136

Sheriff Richard Marks caught in a pensive mood at Father Damien's chapel as he recounts stories of Kalaupapa's past.

These lean-tos were just enough to keep off the wind and the weather. When someone died, the first occupant to take over was the new owner.

Well, it seemed that an old lady had the shack under this L'iang L'iang Tree that is now there. That was the location of it. One day she was found with her head bashed in, dead. No one knew who had done it except that there was one guy who was so tough and so bad that he let nothing stand in the way of what he wanted. Everyone was terrified of him, so when they found her brutally murdered, people were hesitant to go over into her place, but he wasn't and it was suspected that he had done her in. He moved in that same day. Nothing happened at first, but that night there was a scream that would wake the dead. Everyone heard it and came running out. They all saw this same guy take off yelling his head off and running all the way into the next valley. He was naked, no clothes on at all, and down on all fours like an animal. He was so incoherent that no one could make sense of what he was saying. He was in this state for a couple of days while nobody could get near him. Then he died a horrible howling death.

Since then and all down through the years, many people have reported seeing an old woman sitting or maybe standing under the L'iang L'iang tree. Some who have seen her have never heard of the legend or known of the happenings of the place. It is said that she comes to warn people of danger, real or imminent, but whatever her mission she continues to appear to both residents and visitors alike. Sometimes she is seen during the day and sometimes at night, but no one who lives around here will ever visit this part of the island after dark. It just isn't done.

The Haunted Lighthouse

Jutting off of the northern coast of the island of Molokai on Makanalua Point stands a lighthouse with the strongest beacon in the Pacific. Erected in 1909 near the leper colony of Kalaupapa, the lighthouse has been watching over seamen for seventy-five years.

The lighthouse at Kalaupapa rises majestically before the 1,600-foot high cliffs that isolate the peninsula from Upper Molokai.

Hanohano Kalaupapa I ka'u ika

I ka hale kukui kau mai luna
Pa'iwa hikihele ko'u moe 'ana
I ka malamalama kupanaha I ke ao uli.

Hana mai ka uwila I kona mana
Ahuwale Mikahala a e ku ana
Kilakila Enoka ke ku mai
Pailaka akamai I kau ike
A he ui a he ninau ia
O wai keia hale kukui?

O ka hale kukui o Kalaupapa
E hoopakele ana I ke ola o na moku.
He loke pepeiao wale no ko'e.

Akahi a ike maka I kona nani
Ike kanaka I kona nani
I ka huila makeneki e niniu ana
Malamalama ka hikina me ke komohana
Ahuwale Kalwao me Kalaupapa.

Haina ia ka puana.
O ka hale kukui o Kalaupapa.

J.K. Mokumaia

140

In Praise of Makanalua Lighthouse

Distinguished is Kalaupapa in my sight,
With the lighthouse standing above it.
Startled, perturbed is my sleep
By the wondrous brightness in the vault of the heavens.

The electricity does its wondrous power.
There stands the inter-island steamer Mikahala
Majestic is Enoch standing there
Skillful pilot to my view
And it is a query, a question
Who is this lighthouse?

The lighthouse of Kalaupapa,
Saving the lives of the vessels.
I had only hearsay,

This is the first time that I have seen its splendor.
Men see its splendor,
The spinning magnetic wheel,
Bright are the east and the west,
In plain view are Kalawao and Kalaupapa.

Told is the theme,
The lighthouse of Kalaupapa.

(translation by Theodore Kelsey)

The following story is a personal experience that happened to my son David and I during a trip to Molokai over Christmas break in December 1983.

It was a glorious Hawaiian morning as our six-seater Cessna made a wide circle over the peninsula preparatory to landing at Kalaupapa Airport. My son was home from the University of Michigan for Christmas break and we were flying to Molokai for the day. I had visited Kalaupapa before and wished to share this special experience with David. It was to be even more special than each of us anticipated.

Richard Marks, the sheriff of Kalaupapa and local guide par excellence, was to meet us at the airport for a personal tour at ten. However, we were early when our small plane touched down at nine o'clock. After disembarking, we looked around and decided that we had time for a hike to the old lighthouse, which loomed from a hill about a quarter of a mile from the airport.

The author's son, David Thompson, at the base of the Molokai lighthouse.

The morning was breathtaking in its beauty. The clear blue sky was cloudless. Noisy seabirds rose into the air with a great screeching and flapping of wings as we approached. Tiny purple wildflowers mingled with yellow and gold blossoms and a dusty green sea plant covered the lava rocks. The lighthouse shone dazzling white in the morning sun like the beacon it had been for so many years. I noticed cattle grazing at the foot of the hill. They seemed undismayed at our approach. I took deep breaths of the fresh sea air. It felt good to be away from the traffic and crowds of Oahu, the island visible across the sea. It was wonderful to be on holiday and I felt happy, content.

We easily hiked the little hill to the lighthouse. I noticed odd conformations of old lava rock walls winding up the side of the hill in a kind of maze and wondered if they could be the remains of an ancient *heiau.* We paused at the top of the hill to catch our breath and to admire the panorama of sky and sea that sparkled all around us. There was a deserted shack with derelict walls and peeling paint next to the base of the tower. It was forlorn, but so picturesque that I took several photographs from different angles. I then turned the camera towards my son who was exploring the concrete apron that surrounded the base of the tower.

"David, stand there and let me snap a shot of you from this angle!" I called to him.

Although my son was twenty-two, he had always been a roamer when exploring new places and he was just as hard to catch now as when he was growing up. I tried to take his picture at the base of the lighthouse with the sea in the background, but he became increasingly restless and wouldn't stay in one place long enough to snap the shutter.

He finally stood still long enough for me to point the lens skyward from the ground, catching his tall figure standing directly above on the concrete apron with the soaring shaft of the lighthouse behind him. It was an odd shot, but I felt compelled to take it. It had just come into focus when a very strange and clear thought popped into my mind: the figure of a man looking down at us from the top of the lighthouse! Of course, my physical eyes saw nothing and I wondered why such a weird thought had even entered my mind as my finger pressed the button on the camera.

"Hey Mom," David said, off again, "I'm going to hike down to the beach."

"Okay," I replied, "I'll just sit here and catch my breath."

I sat down on the corner of the concrete apron to relax; I took a few deep breaths and let my mind wander just to enjoy the beauty of the scene. Only a minute or two had passed when I felt my mood began to change and a distinct sadness began to creep over me. At first I thought it was my imagination. Outwardly nothing had changed: the sunlight sparkled on that incredibly blue sea, the air smelled just as fresh and the cattle continued to graze contentedly, but a cloud of depression had settled upon me and I consciously remembered the cartoon character in the comic strip "Lil Abner" who used to walk around with a little dark cloud over his head. What's the matter with me, I thought; this is ridiculous!

Just then David jogged up and sat down next to me on the cement apron. A helicopter flew in and we watched as it landed at the airport. We began to talk and the conversation took an odd turn. Personal grievances and petty accusations poured forth, mostly unfounded but deeply upsetting. It was unexpected, intense, and in context of the circumstances made no sense at all. It became a heavy emotional experience although it took no more than ten minutes from beginning to end. I felt tears welling up in my eyes and turned my head away.

I heard David say, "Mom! What's the matter? What's wrong? What's happening, Mom?"

I turned to him and was amazed to see tears in his eyes as well. We stared at each other mystified as to what was happening when we heard an engine approaching and saw a cloud of dust as an old station wagon came lumbering up the dirt road to the lighthouse.

David jumped to his feet. "I'm going to hike back to the airport. See you down there."

The car reached the foot of the lighthouse and I quickly wiped the tears away as I recognized Richard Marks with two uniformed Coastguardsmen carrying tools who were apparently there to fix the light in the tower. Richard and I went down to wait in the car and chat while they did their job.

Twenty minutes later, the Coastguardsmen finished their work and joined us. As we pulled away to return to the airport, I glanced at their faces. One man was young, a *haole* from the Mainland, while the older black man seemed more experienced. Both men looked to be on edge. The lighthouse was receding in the distance and without thinking I turned to Richard and said, "Are there any spooky stories in these parts?"

Richard eyed me sharply and gave a laugh.

"Oh boy, are there!" he said. "That old lighthouse back there is haunted by the ghost of a workman who fell to his death just as they were putting the finishing touches on the tower. I see him all the time."

The Coastguardsmen exchanged quick glances and there was a pause. Then one of them rolled his eyes and said, "Man, that place sure is haunted! I heard *him* talking back there just a few minutes ago."

The younger man nodded in agreement. "Yep. I heard *him* too."

I turned to face them as we barreled down the dusty road. "Do you mean to say that you guys just heard a ghost back there a few minutes ago?"

They looked at each other again.

"We sure did," said the older man. "We both heard *him* up in the tower. He was talking to us, but there was nobody there."

I remembered the impression I had had of a man looking down at David and me from the top of the lighthouse as I took my son's picture. He wasn't there either.

"Yeah," Richard cut in, "There was a guy killed there years ago back when they were building the lighthouse. He still hangs around. I've seen him many times up on the tower usually just before sunset. He always comes out from that side right there..." He pointed out the window of the car to the left of the lighthouse. "...And walks around to the other side on the right and leans over the railing where he fell. Then he disappears. He fell right there."

Richard pointed to the exact spot where David and I had been sitting. I felt a chill in the back of my neck as he continued with his story.

"My wife and daughters spent the night in the cottage by the tower there not long ago. Ha! They won't go near the place now, not one of them! Seems this guy was quite famous on the island in his time, or maybe infamous is more like it. He was a Hawaiian; young, handsome, big, strong, loved to drink and party, and just loved the women. He was a daring kind of guy with his work and was just putting the finishing touches on the tower railing when he slipped and fell to his death."

"They carried his body to the cottage over there and put it in the bedroom. Then they called to report the accident to the state health department in Honolulu. They told 'em they would have to have an autopsy before they could move the body. Imagine! A guy falls three hundred feet from the top of a lighthouse and kills himself and they have to have an autopsy to prove how he did it! Bunch of clowns. Anyway, he lay in the cottage for six days and six nights before they finally got here from Honolulu and took him away. Ever since, people staying in the cottage—it's a kind of guesthouse now—have reported

The cabin at the base of Kalaupapa Lighthouse where the workman was taken after being killed in a fall.

hearing noises and seeing things. Sometimes they actually see this guy and he bothers them, like with my daughters."

"The two of them were sleeping in the bedroom, the same room where his body lay for so many days so long ago. Now both of my girls are not skittish. In fact they never believed any of this stuff before. During the night, however, one of them woke up screaming that there was a man choking her. She swore that there was a man in the bed on top of her with his hands around her neck. Her sister told her to cut it out, that she was having a nightmare, and to go back to sleep, but a few minutes later the same thing happened to her. They both went running out to their mother who was sleeping in the living room. Now my wife is pure Portuguese and—believe me—nothing gets to her! She calmed the girls down and told them they were both having bad dreams and she let them crawl in bed with her. The three of them settled down to pass the rest of the night. It wasn't long before the same thing happened to the mother and she woke up screaming. They all agreed later that they felt a man in bed with them and that he was on top of them. He must still like the women. I've stayed in the cottage many nights and he never bothered me!"

"Anyway, my family ran out of there at 3 o'clock in the morning and they won't go back again. Not one of them will darken the door of that place. So many visitors have reported similar happenings. And, you know, the hill the lighthouse is built on was very sacred in ancient times. It was a heiau then, one of the most sacred. Very special. That's why at first they wouldn't build a lighthouse on it. When they constructed the first lighthouse on the end of the point, it was washed away. When they finally built the one on the top of the hill they had all kinds of trouble with the construction and then finally this guy was killed."

"Many the time," Richard continued, "that I've seen a man's figure up on the top of the lighthouse just at dusk when the light is timed to go on. He always comes from the left side, walks around the light, and is silhouetted for a moment in front of it. He's always bent over as if he's looking for something and he always comes in from the same direction."

The older Coastguardsman broke in. "The door is right there to the left. That's where the voice was coming from."

I turned to him and we introduced ourselves.

"I'm Ed Duty and this is Matt Livingston."

"I'm Judi Thompson," I said. "What exactly did you guys experience back there just now?"

Matt answered.

"When I first went in there to fix the breaker, I was down on the bottom and Ed was in the top. At least, I thought he was. I could hear a voice talking, but I couldn't understand what it was saying and I thought it was Ed telling me to turn the breaker on. I really couldn't hear what was being said. I only knew I heard voices and I answered him back. A few minutes later, Ed called down and told me to turn the breaker on and right then I realized that it wasn't Ed that I was hearing before. It sounded far off and kind of muffled, like a conversation between two people. You could hear them talking back and forth, but it didn't sound like it was right here. It sounded like it was halfway up. It was a man's voice—or maybe two men—that I heard and they were carrying on a conversation, but you couldn't understand what they were saying. I really thought it was Ed calling down from above. I can distinguish between the wind in the lighthouse and voices and these were definitely voices. After Ed really called down, I realized that it wasn't him before and I thought 'whoa… there's somebody else in here!' After Ed came down, I told him what I had heard and he said that he had heard it too."

Ed broke in to say, "Have you ever been inside a hollow building when you hear a bunch of echoes? This sounds like the last echo. You could hardly understand what was being said. It's like an echo, but not exactly. There are a lot of dead birds up there, but it's not a bird and it's not the wind. *It's a voice.* You just can't understand what it is saying. It's strange, but once you've heard it so many times, you just get used to it and try not to pay attention."

"Have you heard this kind of thing before?" I asked.

"Yeah, me and the chief porter, we heard it one day. We both heard the same thing. Once you've heard it, you try not to pay attention. I had heard it before at the lighthouse on Cape Kumukahi on the Big Island. When the 1960 volcano erupted, the lava separated and went around the lighthouse. You can go on top of the lighthouse and see a path where it went around it and didn't touch the lighthouse itself. It was beautiful. The only damage to the tower was the paint blistering from the intense heat. The lava measured forty feet thick and destroyed a nearby village including the lighthouse keeper's quarters. Local Hawaiians claim that Pele spared the tower. There is a little tombstone about ten feet from the lighthouse. I'm not sure if the keeper is under the lava or not, but most likely he is as he didn't want to leave. It's not like this lighthouse here. It's like a little house sitting on a big structure. When I went inside, I heard people talking and when I went outside, there was nobody there. Other guys have experienced it over there too. I took a young guy over there for the first time. He didn't know any of this so he wasn't expecting it. He said, "I heard something," and I replied, "you're going to hear a lot every time you come out here!'"

"So you travel the islands all the time depending on what needs to be done?" I asked.

"No, we get a message at the office if a light goes out. If we can't fly a plane in there, we have to take a helicopter like today. Usually, I fly commercial like Hawaiian Air or Aloha Airlines."

"Do you officially report these happenings?"

"Usually not," Ed said, "although the files are packed full of reports over the years. They keep it quiet. What are they going to do about it? After awhile it gets so commonplace it's taken for granted. New people come on duty and the navigation team around here experiences it so often that it just gets to be normal. It's like, 'well, this lighthouse is haunted.' Oh, yeah? Sure. Okay. Actually there are just two lighthouses in Hawaii that I have heard voices in myself: the Molokai lighthouse we just left and the one at Cape Kumukahi."

We had reached the airport and David was waiting for us. As I got out of the van, I said, "David, a man fell off of the lighthouse when they were building it years ago..."

He finished my sentence for me. "Yeah, right where we were sitting. It's haunted, isn't it, Mom?"

We looked at each other and knew the reason for our tears.

June Gutmanis' Ghosties

June Gutmanis was a writer, researcher, consultant, and teacher of Hawaiian and Pacific cultural and historic topics. Her publications include Kahuna La'au Lapa'au, a study of ancient Hawaiian herbal medicine; Life Histories of Native Hawaiians, a collection of oral histories of kapuna, older Hawaiian people; Na Pule Kahiko, a collection of pre-European Hawaiian prayers; and Maui, Our Common Ancestor. She shared these experiences on the lanai of her charming "sugar shack" in Waianae in August of 1983.

The Ghost in the Tri-Corner Hat

For a number of years, we lived on top of the hill near the highway leading into the heart of Kailua on Oahu. There is a *heiau* across the road and there are several in the area. The land seemed to have been heavily inhabited since ancient times. I used

June Gutmanis relaxes on her lanai with her black cat.

151

to dig up *opihi* shells several feet down into the earth when I was planting. I found quite a bit of *opihi* up there, probably refuse from a house long gone.

Strange things happened during the years we lived there. We kept horses and when the kids would go to feed them in the paddock, they would sometimes come back to the house talking about the music they had heard: drums, flutes, and singing. No one could figure out where it was coming from, as this kind of activity would not fit any of our neighbors! (It was quite a *haole* professional kind of neighborhood.)

From time to time, I sensed an actual presence in the house. I felt as though an entity were really there. I would be talking to someone and would suddenly experience an awareness of becoming very body-tense. Frequently the other person would glance about and ask if someone had come in. Later as I was beginning to relax, my companion would say, "They've left now." That mutual awareness before the experience was verbalized is a kind of confirmation.

The first physical manifestation occurred during the visit of a friend, Jim Lawrence, a student at Chaminade College. His mother was a fashion designer who had held shows for *EBONY Magazine*. His background gave him an acute fashion consciousness of fabric and design. On this particular day, he had gone to feed the horses and when he returned, he had come in abruptly and just plopped down in an armchair. Now Jim is African American, but his skin had turned color and you would have to say that he was very pale. I said, "What's the matter, Jim?" and it was several moments before he was able to answer.

It seemed that he had been taking feed from the tack room when he had seen a figure standing by the corner of the building. Because of his upbringing in the fashion world, he was able to give a detailed description of what the man was wearing. He described the figure of a man wearing a shirt with long full sleeves made out of a fabric that looked like silk, heavy fabric pants, and a tri-corner hat. He went on to describe the fabric in detail and the rest of the costume, including the shoes and socks. It was a fully dressed, solid entity he had witnessed that then proceeded to disappear before his eyes! He thought it must have been the neighbor, a Dr. Bennett, but somehow this explanation failed to explain the mysterious, abrupt disappearance.

About a year later, I held a New Years Eve party and the ghost in the tri-corner hat made another appearance as an uninvited guest. At least three people at the party saw him. The guest with the most vivid description was an artist who had glanced out of the window and had noticed a man in a white silk shirt and a three-corner hat running across the lawn when he suddenly disappeared before her eyes. She was so upset by what she had seen that it was several months before she would talk to anyone about it. She thought she was going crazy when she clearly saw a figure running across the lawn that suddenly wasn't there!

Another guest saw the same figure run across the grass and suddenly disappear, but he initially dismissed it as his having too much to drink. Then there was our Russian-Greek friend who would never dance with anyone but, as the Greeks are wont to do, loved to dance by himself. He was out dancing on the lawn away from everybody else when he saw the figure. All three must have seen the same figure at about the same time. It was interesting to note that two of these people had grown up with a lot of experience with clothing and fabric, so they were able to observe and describe the clothing on the figure vividly.

That was my elegant ghost on the hill in Kailua.

Shaseda

In the Japanese language there is a word called *shaseda*. It means that when a person dies, he comes to tell you. I have a story for you. It happened just a few weeks ago. I received a call from my daughter and a close friend on the Big Island. They were complaining that "somebody" had visited them the previous night at 4:30 a.m. Now my friend JoAnn sleeps sounder than anyone I've ever seen, but whatever—or whomever—it was woke her up. Both women clearly heard footsteps walking through their home, heard it kick something, pause, and then continue walking. When they got up and turned on the light, there was nothing—and *no one*—there.

Now this is a tiny place and the odd thing is JoAnn has nine Great Danes and three or four other dogs and if anyone sets foot on the property, the dogs get very upset and start barking until you can't hear yourself think. There is a carport and the rest of the house is open so the slightest disturbance would have awakened the dogs and set them off. Not one dog barked.

A couple of days later, JoAnn called again and during the conversation mentioned that a friend had committed suicide. We discussed what to say to the survivors and she said that he had owed them $3,000.

Three days after that, I received another phone call from the Big Island. It was JoAnn. She said, "I know who came to visit us. It was Kimo, our friend who owed us the money. We found out he killed himself at 4:30 a.m. the same night as our visitor." He had made a promise he had not lived to keep.

Now this was a classic example of what is termed by H. Carrington as "death coincidence" because it happened in documented segments with more then one witness and there were no presumptions. The timing was uncannily perfect.

A similar occurrence had happened to me just before this. I can verify the timing exactly. Theodore Kelsey, the well-known historian of Hawaiiana who lived with us, had suffered a slight stroke. I had been home almost constantly taking care of him as he convalesced. It was Saturday afternoon. "Hawaii 5-0" reruns play on television at 4 p.m. and I had planned to turn it on for Mr. K. to watch. I thought he might notice a familiar Hawaiian scene, which would interest him and perhaps spark a conversation or start a train of thought. It was between 3 and 3:30 when I was walking across the room to turn on the TV when suddenly a mutual friend, Mr. Cathcart, popped into my mind most strongly. In fact it was such a strong impression that I started into my workroom to write a note to him. Then I remembered that it was the weekend and the letter wouldn't go out until Monday's mail, so I put it off until later in the day.

Mr. Kelsey must have picked up on my thought because all of a sudden he began to talk about "the old man."

"What old man?" I asked him.

"The old man who goes to the bathroom," he replied in a somewhat confused manner. "Where is he? He has a message for you."

"What message?"

But Mr. K. did not answer.

The television was still playing when we heard on the six o'clock news that Mr. Cathcart had been burned in a fire. He had died at 3:14 p.m. that same day.

As soon as I saw the news story I wondered if Mr. Cathcart's dogs had escaped the fire. I had once promised him that is anything ever happened to him I would take care of his two dogs. A couple of phone calls let me know the two dogs had survived. With the help of one of my daughters I was able to go into town and get them out of his collapsed and burned out home. They are now happily part of my animal family.

I wonder if he was reminding me of my promise?

Theodore Kelsey was an important figure in Hawaiiana. We were fortunate to have known him. Mr. Kelsey never talked about any psychic experiences of his own. He was interested in the paranormal as his father warned him way back in the 1920s that he should leave psychic experimentations alone and concentrate on marrying a nice girl and raising a family! How the psychic would interfere with getting married I don't know.

I do know that he once wanted to use an ouiji board to check on some points of clarification for the Kumulipo he was translating. He and my daughter were trying it and they were getting simple answers... in Hawaiian! Three-letter words mostly, but Kelsey wasn't satisfied. He wanted sentences. The interesting thing is my daughter did not and does not speak Hawaiian so she wasn't consciously manipulating it. They tried it twice before they gave up.

Ghost Riders

My husband—Herr Gutmanis—was very practical and down to earth. We were living in Koko Head or Hawaii Kai before Kaiser. We had this long room in our house that was a combination living and dining room. One night he was working at the table there. It was about 2 a.m. and he was reading by lamplight. All of a sudden, he looked up and his face went totally white. He said, "Who's riding the horses?"

"No one!" I replied.

He repeated, "Are the children riding the horses?"

Now the children were all in bed sound asleep. I *knew* it wasn't the children riding the horses.

"It's 2 a.m.!" I snapped.

"Well," he said slowly, "I hadn't thought about the time, but *somebody* just rode by our window. I saw them..."

Our picture window was very high up so in order for a figure—or even the torso of a figure—to be seen, it would have had to been on horseback. My husband swore to his dying day that he clearly saw a figure go riding by our window and there was no one there.

He never did make fun of ghosts after that.

A Little Night Music

It was New Years Eve in the mid 1970s. My daughter and I had said to heck with a New Years Eve party and we decided to take a bunch of friends camping. We got a bunch together and went off to Kaena Point. I had been interested in the spirit-leaping-off places around there and had found out where one of the points were supposed to be. When we reached the spot where it was located, I asked that we camp there. I did not say anything about the history of the place.

We arrived about three or four in the afternoon and set up camp. The kids gathered wood and we had a good cookout. We were without lamps so by ten o'clock we all settled down and went to bed.

We had quite a cross-section of kids there: a couple of *haoles* from the Mainland, some local kids, and some part-Hawaiian. The next morning, *all* of the kids were talking. Every one of them had heard music playing during the night. I told them all to be still and I questioned them. I wanted it to be an objective questioning without feeding them any information at all, so I asked them things like, "What did you hear?" and "What kind of music was it?"

They all agreed on the same things. They had all heard singing and what sounded like drums and a flute or a recorder. (Some of them were into recorders at the time.) None of the adults heard anything, but every one of the kids had heard it. There was definitely nobody else around for miles. No one passed us on the old road or arrived at any time. We were alone.

When I got back to the house, I happened to check a calendar with the phases of the moon and sure enough. The night of our campout was the Night of Kane, one of the times when the Night Marchers are supposed to appear.

157

Ghost Dogs

Have you heard of the Ghost Dog of Pupukea? When we lived in Pupukea, we had a neighbor who was a Coast Guard Chief. He only believed in what he could see and touch, as he was really pragmatic and very tough. We lived across the street from his place, but there was an old path that had once gone along the side of both lots. Our property was about three or four feet higher than his, so there was a light rise.

One day during the Christmas season, he was in his yard and suddenly he saw a Hawaiian man and a white dog standing on the path right in front of him. It was in broad daylight and he saw them clearly. After looking him over, they both evaporated right before his eyes. They simply disappeared.

Well, he swore over and over again that he had seen them and he believed that it was real. He said that if it hadn't happened to him personally, he never would have believed such a thing, but that it did happen and now he did believe it. Again, it was at the same time of the month when the Night Marchers were said to appear.

Timing seems to have something to do with these happenings. When we bought the house at Koko Head, a little dog came with the property. We were told that he was a nice little dog and no trouble to keep, but that once a month he would have a barking spell. It was different than his usual barking. When that happened, we were supposed to tie him up and he would quit.

Sure enough once a month, at the same time each month, the little dog would start to bark on and on and on. Soon all the other dogs in the neighborhood would be barking too.

Well, I wasn't into tying dogs up and I also found out that it didn't matter if you tied him or not as he kept on barking anyway.

He always went to one particular spot in the yard and barked and barked at it as though he saw something, but there was nothing. He would quit after awhile at about the same time until the next month.

I would always check, really check, to be sure there wasn't a mongoose or something. It was always the same place and always between the eighth and the thirteenth of the month. I began to realize that other dogs in the neighborhood also followed this barking pattern. After awhile I was given a goat and tied him up at night on the same spot. I let him loose during the day, but tied him at night as he liked to wander over in my neighbor's yard and devour his prize orchids. You know after the goat moved in, the barking stopped! I don't know if the spirits didn't like the goat smell or what, but it all cleared out.

When we moved to Kailua and later to Pupukea, however, the pattern remained the same. I kept track of this pattern myself for almost ten years. When I taught classes in Hawaiiana for over two years, I asked my students to write down the dates of certain nights if they noticed the dogs beginning to bark. The students would always write down dates between the eighth and the thirteenth. It has nothing to do with the lunar calendar and I haven't been able to figure it out.

Collectable Tales

Contributed by Dr. Katharine Luomala. Collected by Stanley Koki as told by Dorothy Uyehara. The story of Georgie Mama's son was heard by Dorothy when she was a child growing up in the Kam IV Road area of Kalihi, a small pig-raising community comprised mostly of Japanese immigrants and their families. Mama Georgie was an actual person who lived on Lower Kam IV Road. She had the reputation of possessing supernatural power that she did not hesitate to use whenever provoked.

The Skeleton in the Cave

This **ACTUALLY** happened.

One day Georgie Mama's son went up to the mountains with another boy. In a cave they found the skeleton of a human being. It was a complete skeleton like one used in biology classes. Georgie Mama's son said, "Look, a skeleton!" The other boy was frightened and turned his face from it. He wanted to leave the cave immediately, but Georgie Mama's son refused. He wanted the skeleton and he forced his friend to help him carry it down with him to his house. Georgie Mama's son put the skeleton under the house.

That night he was very tired so he went to bed early. Late at night when the grandfather's clock in the hallway struck twelve, Georgie Mama's son was awakened by the touch of a cold hand on his arm. He opened his eyes quickly to see who it was, but he saw no one. He thought that maybe it was all in his imagination, so he went back to sleep. But he woke up again when he felt a cold hand touch his throat.

He sprang up and put the light on quickly. There was no one. The house was empty except for him. Everything was quiet except for the ticking of the grandfather clock, so he turned off the light and went

Dr. Katharine Luomala in her office at the University of Hawaii.

back to sleep. He was awakened again by the rattling of all the walls of the house. They rattled and shook as if a huge being was trying to tear it off its foundations. The boards creaked and groaned. Georgie Mama's son thought it was due to a storm, but when he dashed to the window he saw that the wind was not blowing outside. Everything was silent and still. Not a leaf moved.

Fear froze his blood and made his hair tingle at the back of his neck. He rushed downstairs to see the skeleton for he suspected a connection between the strange things that were happening and the skeleton under the house. He found out that a dog had eaten part of the skull.

He knew now what was troubling him. He began shivering as if it was snowing outside and he had nothing to wear for he knew that he was not alone in the house. Although he could see no one, he knew that somebody else was in the house with him. So he got a flashlight and ran over to his friend's house. He told his friend everything that had happened and that very night the two of them went up the mountain to return the skeleton. For miles down you could see the light from their flashlight moving steadily up the mountain as if it were a firefly moving up and up, until it disappeared into the cave.

The Ghosts of Mana

Collected by Edward Y. Hokama from B. Nakagawa around 1954.

In a lonely place called Mana on the island of Hawaii, there is a small settlement of wooden houses that are no longer occupied. Near the houses is a graveyard. Here all the members of the famous Parker family of the Parker Ranch are buried. Until a few months ago, there lived only one family in the Mana district. That was the family of the caretaker of Mana whose name is Mr. Aoki. Mr. Aoki lived in this place for many years as caretaker and only recently moved out when all the members of his family were going to schools too distant from the area.

There are ghosts in Mana and only Mr. Aoki and his oldest son have been able to see them. The rest of the family cannot see them. Many times other families have tried to move into the area. Each time, after a few days, weeks, or months of horrible experiences, the people have hastily moved out again. There have been reports of invisible "ghosts" grasping the throats of members of the newcomer families and many other similar physical assaults by unseen forces.

Living not too far from this place rather a long time ago, another family had an interesting experience. It was after the beginning of World War II during the occupation of the islands by members of the United States Armed Forces. The Army post was in that area and therefore they had a sentry guarding the road close to where this family lived.

One night the guard suddenly saw a huge white form. He commanded the figure to stop. It didn't. He obviously knew this was no human being, so he opened fire with his M-a rifle. He emptied his clip of ammunition, but the form did not fall. It slowly disappeared. In his excitement, the guard didn't realize that the figure was directly in line with the home of the family. The bullets tore holes in the roof of the house as the members of the family became alarmed by the din of the impact of lead tearing through their wooden roof. After that incident, there were always two sentries on duty in that area and to this day, no one dares live in Mana.

The Invisible Hand

Collected by William T. Kikuchi from Richard Paglina in 1961.

On the island of Oahu at Waimalu Valley near Aiea, there lived many truck farmers, mostly Japanese. The only Hawaiian family lived near the single gate that allowed passage to and from the valley. In this home site, the Hawaiian farmer and his Hawaiian wife lived with twelve of their own children in addition to eight boys and two girls who were unofficially *hanai* or adopted by them.

The Hawaiian house, a modest little home, had features that incorporated both the *haole* and the Hawaiian form. In addition to the house plan, there was a kitchen separate from the house, but still under one roof (typically Hawaiian), which had a bare dirt floor, four walls, a few benches, seats, plus a sink and a wood-burning stove. The family ate together in the kitchen enjoying their meal after a hard day in the fields.

One of the daughters was washing the dishes after eating one night when she saw the tail of a rat wiggling through the cracks in the wall in front of her. She didn't take much notice of the tail at first, but she splashed water on it. To her annoyance, however, the tail kept coming back. She then grabbed a meat cleaver and was about to strike at the tail. Before she could swing, a hand—or something like a hand—reached out and grasped her throat. She screamed, which scared all the children who were eating at the time. She then fell to the ground bleeding profusely with a large wound under her jaw.

Her father perceived the cause of the attack on his daughter as "Chokeneck" and told his wife that all of the children must stay in the house. He said that he was going to undress and run around the house and in time he would call out for her to quickly open the door to let him in.

He ran outside and immediately began to run around the house. Noises were heard as if someone were really chasing him. He ran for what seemed to be a long time. Finally he called to his wife to let him in and she did as he had instructed. He ran in and fell down in exhaustion. In his hands was a weed, an herb for his daughter's wound. This process was repeated for several nights. Finally, with the herb's medicinal power, the wound healed, but to this day the daughter has a large prominent scar below her jaw.

The Story of Napoleon Kaloli'i Kapukui

Dr. Mary Kawena Pukui was an author, historian, lexicographer, lecturer, translator, consultant, hula and chant instructor, genealogist, and composer of "No Keaha?", "Kipukai," "Kalehua I Milila," "Laupahoehoe Hula," and others. This collection is a curious one because it was "collected from a collector" in a sense and shared by Kenji Kalolii Pomroy.

Mary is my aunt and has been a curator for Bishop Museum, a translator of books both in and out of Hawaiian. She has collaborated in the writing of books that have tried to save what is left of the Hawaiian culture. This particular genealogy is close to me because I was named after this uncle, Kaloli'i. In Hawaiian culture, a genealogy is not just a family tree; it's your mana, your strength. It's where you come from and to what you return.

Kona, Hawaii. A storm at sea had deprived her of a husband in August of that year. She was left with her parents-in-law and four children. Grief over her husband soon unbalanced her mind and the children found themselves in four different homes. Kaloli'i (who became my husband) was spoken for by Pakekepa Bathsheba Kailikeu, cousin of the boy's dead father, Kapukui. The grandparents watched over this youngest child until he was weaned. Then when his adopted mother took him to Honolulu soon after his first birthday, his paternal grandfather, Kahuamoa, and grandmother, Kauha'akalani, went along to care for the baby.

Kaloli'i was extremely fond of his grandparents, particularly of his grandfather. Very often the old man and small boy would be seen gathering algeroba beans, which the old man sold. Part of the money was always used to buy cakes for the child. The two were inseparable until the grandfather died.

One day in December 1875 (the date was never recorded), a son was born to Kaaimakui, widow of Kapukui of Keauhou.

Kauha'akalani, the grandmother, died when Kaloli'i was about four years of age. He told me that she was ill and unable to get about prior to her death, so he was surprised one late afternoon to see her come out of the house, smile at him, and walk away down the path that ran by the side of the house. He hastened to find his grandfather to tell him that he had seen his grandmother walk away, well and smiling. When the two went to look for her, they found that life had left her body. His grandfather joined her a few years later.

The old man was a fisherman, a lover of the sea as were his forebearers. His only son was also a follower of the sea until it claimed him as its own. Solomon, Kaloli'i's older brother, was a fisherman and a sailor who had traveled to foreign lands. There was "salt water in their blood," as the saying is, and today many of the younger members are heeding the call of the sea.

It was said that the first-born child of my parents-in-law was a shark. The mother, Ka'aimahui, was on her way to Kahalui from Keauhou when she was seized with pain. She sat on the beach to rest and there her child was prematurely born. He showed no animation. Removing her calico undergarment, she wrapped him up in it and hid him away under a *pohuehue* vine. After she felt rested, she proceeded to Kahalui, to the house of relatives. In the late afternoon, she was brought home by horseback. They paused at the spot where she left her baby, but it was gone, undergarment and all. The tide had come up and in receding, removed her hidden bundle. A few weeks later, as she entered the sea at Keauhou, a fish seized her nipples and nursed at her breast. In terror, she tried to push it away, but was warned by a watching relative not to do so for that was the first-born child she had lost. The gods of the sea had changed him from a human form to that of a shark and had given him life. Upon close examination, they found that the skin had the markings of the garment in which he was wrapped.

An interested relative, Manuia, became his *kahu* or his keeper, and would feed him *awa* or bananas. He was said to be a very friendly shark that was never known to harm or annoy anyone.

Years later when the oldest sister, Laie, visited Kona, her hat blew off her head into the sea. She was surprised to see it coming back, pushed along by the nose of a shark, and learned that he was none other than her *hiapo* or first-born brother.

3

Firehouse Ghost Tales

Introduction

I walked into Old Downtown Firehouse on President's Day looking for my initial contact, Dexter Alameida. I learned that he was stationed at Kakaako Firehouse, so I spoke with four other men including Kimo and the Chief. I found the men to be open, interested, and eager to talk about the subject of Chokeneck and other strange happenings. They were most helpful in sharing the best stations for me to visit and I quickly learned that the older firehouses were the richest sources of ghost stories and were, in fact, known for these occurrences. I was advised that the best approach was to simply walk in and state my case. As it was, this initial contact was an interesting source of stories itself. However, all of these stories were second-hand as none of the men I spoke with were personally involved in the incidents related. The main station seemed to have no activity of a supernatural nature, at least none that the men were willing to share. However much activity, some of it recent, was prescribed to the following stations: Station 25 – Nuuanu, Station 9 – Kakaaku, Station 5 – Kaimuki, and Station 3 – Makiki.

I was told that a personal experience was had by Winston Lum who transferred from Nuuanu Station to serve in Administration in downtown Honolulu following a Chokeneck attack. He refused to return to night duty as a fireman in

Nuuanu Station after a choking ghost reportedly grabbed him around the neck and sent him yelling from the back of the building.

Kimo, an experienced fireman in his fifties, said, "You hear these stories and they're just stories, you know, but I've known Winston Lum for many years and when Winston says something happened… well, you have just got to give it credence. When Winston tells it, I gotta listen. He's that kind of guy and he swore it happened to him."

"Yeah, it took the whole crew to calm him down!" a younger fireman chimed in.

"He shot out of the back of that firehouse yelling and screaming bloody murder and he won't set foot in that room again. He won't sleep there. Man, he was spooked!"

The fire chief wandered up just then.

"Yeah, old Winston Lum, he transferred after that. He doesn't work at night now, just nine to five in an office downtown all day long."

"Remember the other guy?" said a third fireman. "The one who was pinned to his cot in Nuuanu Station and couldn't get up with the weight on his chest? It was choking him too."

"Yeah, he slept with *ti* leaves under his bed. Still does, but it didn't stop it," the second fireman replied.

"You mean he used *ti* leaves to ward it off?" I asked.

"Yeah. He even had the bed blessed by an old Hawaiian *kahuna*. A Catholic priest too. With the holy water and the salt water and the *ti* leaves and the whole thing, but no good."

"It didn't stop then?" I persisted.

"Finally an old Hawaiian said to move the bed. It was right by the door." He turned to the second fireman. "Remember? He said it was in the middle of some kind of pathway or trail to the mountains. And the guy said why should I move my bed? But when the stuff kept happening, he did."

"And it stopped then?" I queried.

"Yep. Then it stopped."

The young fireman spoke up. "But some of these things happened recently. I just heard about it. You know, up in Kaimuki at Station 5."

"Oh yeah! The boys had just returned from fighting a fire and there is this figure standing in the kitchen and they all saw him. The whole bunch saw him and he was heating up food. Food all over the kitchen, piping hot! And when they walked into the kitchen, he disappeared right before their eyes. Just like that. But then there was all this food left and it was all hot, so they ate it."

I thanked the men and left.

I planned to visit the firehouses recommended to me and interview the firemen there on tape. Most of these visits will probably be at night as time for this activity is limited. It will be interesting to see whether or not the time of day would affect the storytelling in any way. I plan to tape as spontaneously a telling as possible sans manipulative questioning and comments in order to obtain a "pure" taping. My daughter, Rebecca, has asked to accompany me.

Wylie Station #25

Chokeneck

The first interview conducted for Supernatural Hawaii was with the firemen of Wylie Station #25 in Nuuanu Valley, Honolulu. One of the oldest of the Hawaiian Fire Stations, Nuuanu Station was well known for its unusual experiences. My daughter, Rebecca, recorded the following experience for a term paper at Punahou School when she was seventeen years old.

Everybody loves a good ghost story. When I found out that my mother was going to be doing research on "Firehouse Ghost Tales" for a book she was writing, I jumped at the chance to tag along for her interviews. It turned out to be more than interesting. She was expecting to record second-hand stories, folklore per se, rarely encountering a first-person experience. However, the very first fire station we visited had a first-person experience that would send shivers up your spine! I went with her many times after that—almost every session offers a first-person experience, so many in fact that she has expanded her book from a small pamphlet tentatively entitled "Firehouse Ghost Tales" to a full-fledged book.

We have joined firemen in their wardroom nibbling on oatmeal cookies and drinking tea while shivers ran up and down our spines, perched in the dark on the end of a pier by Fireboat Station while ghostly tales were spun, and sat on lava rock walls under a mango tree beneath a full Halloween moon while tales of a phantom given to choking firemen at night were related.

One of the most popular tales we encountered in all of our interviews involves the choking ghost. "Chokeneck," as they call him, is a reoccurring motif. It seems clear to us that there is more than one Chokeneck. A few men claimed to have seen a dark shadowy figure, while others only felt a sensation of fingers around their necks choking them while they tried to cry out and were unable to do so. One man described it as a tall dark man with blood red feet. Whether they actually saw it or not, all have described the exact same experience.

All of the men we talked to were sober, steady, intelligent, stable men, strong and able, and not given to excitable or hysterical reactions. In fact, their very training was dedicated to calm thinking and steady reflex action. Yet these were the very men telling us about the weight that would jump on their chests in the middle of the night paralyzing them for several seconds or minutes.

One man afflicted with the common experience called "Chokeneck" by the firemen was the Hawaii State Karate Champ. After listening to big, strong, practical firemen tell their stories, I believe it's apparent that SOMETHING indeed is happening, *some phenomena is occurring*. All of the details appear to be consistent throughout the stories we have heard thus far.

The thing I find strange is that out of all of these victims of Chokeneck, only one man died. No one is sure as to what caused his death, but it appears that he had a heart attack during the night. Some say that he had come in contact with Chokeneck before.

One theory that could explain these instances has to do with energy. This theory is a part of metaphysics. It says that a person's center of energy is located in the middle of their chest. When the men felt a great pressure on their chests, it is possible that a supernatural being is "recharging" itself by draining the energy from these people. This explains why no one was killed and why all reported feeling feeble and weak after the attack. It also explains why Hawaiians are not the only ones plagued by Chokeneck.

The very first firemen we interviewed were stationed at Nuuanu. This was our first interview and we didn't quite know how to go about it. We decided just to introduce ourselves and tell them exactly why we were there. The looks on some of their faces suggested that we were quite crazy. After a few minutes of embarrassed snickering, a couple of expressions changed to more seriousness. Now we got down to business.

Nuuanu being one of the oldest firehouses was well-known for its unusual experiences. When asked if anyone had any first-hand experience with the supernatural, one fireman, Jan Yasuda, was reluctant in answering. After a short while, he started to relax and told us his story.

He was sleeping one night when he suddenly woke up and found that he couldn't breathe. Struggling to move, he said that he felt this tremendous pressure on his chest like someone was sitting on him. His eyes were wide open yet he saw nothing. After about eight seconds of this, the pressure stopped and he was flung off the bed onto the hard floor. This incident occurred three different times and then quit. All three times happened while he was resting in bed.

Another man in the station was actually able to see the ghost. While everyone else was sleeping, he would yell, "Do you see him?" The man would then become paralyzed in his bed and make noises like he was being choked. A lot of the other men thought he was just having a bad dream so they would go back to sleep. Still others who had experienced this before too didn't know what to do about it. It was over in a few minutes anyway. This man described the ghost as a big tall black man, dark all over. From then on, their choking ghost was known as "Black Man."

At first it was thought that things like this only happened to Hawaiians or part-Hawaiians, but Jan's phenomenon and others have proven that this is not so. Jan Yasuda is pure Japanese. It seemed that location and time of night or day had more to do with the happening than racial background, age, or sex of the person involved. It was also thought that only Hawaiians used *ti* leaves for protection. This is not so either. Many men had *ti* leaves placed under their mattresses to keep spirits away. I found it interesting that *ti* leaves can be seen planted around most of the fire stations. There is a strong credulity that these leaves protect people from evil spirits. At some of the older stations, fire trucks were once used as hearses and they returned from the cemetery to the station covered with *ti* leaves.

One explanation for Jan's story was brought up by a fellow fireman. He mentioned that an ancient Hawaiian trail used by fishermen passed right through the exact room where the men slept. He took us back to show us the room and we noticed that the beds on one side were in direct line with the mountains and the sea. The fishermen's trail seemed to be logical reasoning. Sometimes these ghostly fishermen are called Night Marchers.

As we prepared to leave, the alarm unexpectedly rang and voices shot through the loud speaker. In seconds, the men were on their feet as they jumped on the truck and were off. We were left feeling astonished as coffee still steamed in mugs and a cigarette was left smoking in the ashtray. We could hear the sirens fading in the distance, thus ending our first interview.

As it is, the research for this project is not finished. In fact, we have just begun. The best we can do for now is just to document these stories and present the facts accurately. Several patterns are discernable to any reader concerning matters such as these. This phenomenon is happening as much today as in the past. Certain things—like Chokeneck—reoccur over and over again. People of all ages, different occupations, and racial backgrounds are experiencing these things.

So it is very real.

FIRE!

Wylie Station in Nuuanu Valley on Oahu is infamous among the men of the Hawaii State Fire Department for ghostly happenings. It's located just off the Pali Highway across the street from old Nuuanu Cemetery and the Royal Mausoleum. It's reportedly situated on a trail used by the legendary Night Marchers stretching from the Pali to the sea. Many incidents of Chokeneck have reputedly occurred here.

My daughter Rebecca had accompanied me to visit with the men of Wylie Station to verify the many stories of Chokeneck that had supposedly happened here. As we knocked on the kitchen door and introduced ourselves, explaining our purpose for being there, I noticed that a virtual hedge of ti leaves surrounded the entire building.

We entered and were greeted by a young fireman named Jan Yasuda. When I mentioned the term "Chokeneck," he gave me a funny look.

"Well, yeah, that happened to me," he said.

I was amazed to run into someone who had experienced the phenomena firsthand and I asked him to elaborate.

"It was about four years back when it started," he began, "during the first couple of years I was stationed here. It happened at night, but it also happened in the afternoon. I was taking a nap one day when all of a sudden I felt this thing sitting on my chest like I was having a heart attack or something. I was sound asleep and it woke me up because I couldn't breathe. My eyes were open wide, but I couldn't talk, I couldn't move, I couldn't do anything! I was paralyzed, all stretched out, and scared. Suddenly this weight—this thing—just got off me and I came flying off the bed onto the floor. I was surprised, you know. Wow, what was that? It was a strange sensation like someone sitting on my chest. The weight was mainly on my chest, but it affected my whole body. My eyes were wide open and I remember looking at the floor coming up to meet me as I came flying off the bed. It lasted only a few seconds, maybe eight to ten seconds at most, but it seemed like it lasted a long time. I could see nothing. There was nothing there. It happened three times all within a one-day period, once in the afternoon and twice at night. After that, they left me alone. When I first came here, there were *ti* leaves under the bed. I found them when I turned the mattress over to make up the bed."

The men offered us tea and cookies and we gratefully accepted.

"Exactly what do *ti* leaves do to prevent this kind of thing from happening?" I asked between bites of chocolate chip cookie.

A fireman across the table answered. "They are for protection. You know how vampires are said to keep away from a cross? Hawaiians use *ti* leaves to do the same thing. Priests like Reverend Akaka would bless them and that would accomplish the same thing."

Captain Roy Okuda walked in at that moment. I stood as Jan introduced us and explained our mission.

"I couldn't help overhearing part of your conversation," he said. "Up at Makiki and Kakaako stations, you know, they use the fire trucks as a hearse. When a fireman passes away, they use it to carry them to the grave. Also the truck from this station. When a truck comes back from a funeral, it is virtually covered with *ti* leaves. I remember when I first saw the truck come back from a funeral at Kakaako, I thought what are all these *ti* leaves doing here stuffed all over? They are believed to keep the spirits away, of course."

Another fireman spoke up. "You know a lot of Hawaiians take this very seriously. It's not a joke. I remember one guy I knew scolding my wife years ago. She was joking about the *ti* leaves and he scolded her."

"Up in Makiki some of the guys sleep with *ti* leaves under their mattresses to ward off the same experience," said Captain Okuda. "Especially Hawaiians."

"Watch your step here," Jan said, as he led us into a large room neatly lined with beds.

"Has this building been blessed?" I wondered.

"Oh, most fire stations are blessed. It's the custom," he replied. "This is where my bed is and as far as I know the beds have always been arranged like this." He motioned to a bed near the corner by a big window facing the mountains.

"It doesn't seem to bother with this side at all," he said pointing to the wall by the garage.

"It sure is lined up with the mountains and the sea, isn't it?" I noticed.

"Sure is. I don't know if there is anything to this Night Marcher path theory or not, but it looks like it could have something to do with it by the location of the beds affected. And here's another thing—there's this one particular toilet in the same 'pathway' that jiggles its handle all by itself. It's really weird and there's nothing mechanically wrong with it. It's been checked time and time again. It's right here."

Stepping around the doorway to the bathroom, we were treated to a view of a haunted toilet. Sure enough, it was exactly in line with the bed, the window, and the mountain. Jan leaned over and jiggled the handle hard. It made a definite rattling sound.

"See, it takes some pressure to move that. It's not the wind!" he said as I took one more look around the room with the bed-lined walls.

"I wouldn't be surprised if there are *ti* leaves under most of these mattresses right now!" Jan commented as he led us back into the wardroom.

"Why not?" I responded. "It's good insurance."

"Well, we can't thank you enough for your time," I said.

"No problem," said Jan. "I'm glad somebody is interested enough to ask."

"Very interested," Rebecca and I said together.

"You know these stories and happenings have been around for a long time and..."

Just then a shrill alarm sounded throughout the building. The men jumped to their feet, grabbing helmets and coats and throwing their uniforms on. Voices sounded over a loudspeaker and a siren arose from the garage. The noise was deafening. There was an instantaneous flurry of intense activity and then it was over.

"Got to go!" yelled Jan jumping onto the back of the truck as it roared out of the garage. We saw him wave good-bye as the truck streaked into the street and disappeared.

We heard the siren wail for a minute before dying away in the distance.

The station was deserted as Rebecca and I walked back through the kitchen on our way to the door. Coffee steamed in mugs. There was a cigarette still smoking in an ashtray. The men had literally disappeared within seconds.

Apparitions in the Apparatus Room

This account is from Fireman Winston Lum.

This happened several years ago in 1967. I was stationed at Iwalei, which is in the industrial section of Honolulu, a stone's throw from the Waterfront Fire Station. We had gone to Wylie Station to stand by. "Standing by" is when the entire station is out and another company comes to fill in while they are gone.

It was early in the morning and I was so tired I had slept on the hose bed of the apparatus engine in the garage. It wasn't polite to be sleeping on somebody else's bed and we didn't know how long we were going to be there, so I had just fallen asleep on the wagon. I was lying down and the light was shining out from the kitchen doorway when I suddenly awoke.

There were three figures standing against the light about three feet away looking down at me. I couldn't make out their faces as the light was in back of them, but they were figures or shadows and I was choking. I couldn't lift my arms and I couldn't get up. The figures weren't actually doing anything to me, but I couldn't move at all, not even my head. I could only move my eyes.

I could see the outline of the three bodies. The tallest one was in the middle and he was definitely a man. I'm not sure of the two on the sides as the shadows overlapped. They did not seem to have long hair so perhaps they were all men. I couldn't tell. I thought perhaps the other guys were playing a joke on me, but when I started to speak, nothing would come out. I tried to call to one of the other fellows in the station, but I couldn't make a sound. It was just as if I were paralyzed. It was all very vivid and I was conscious of being wide awake. I told myself that I must be dreaming, but I wasn't. I tried to think logically, but I couldn't dispute that it was happening. Since I couldn't come up with an answer, I thought I'd better just leave it alone.

All of a sudden somebody turned on the light in the apparatus room and that's when everything went back to normal. It all disappeared in a second. Whatever burden was on me, it lifted just like that. When I asked the guy if he heard me yelling, he replied that he hadn't heard anything. He just felt like switching the light on. I found out later that there was only one person in the kitchen at the time and I had definitely seen these three figures.

I didn't feel frightened, I just felt strange. My Chinese side is very logical and my Hawaiian side says well, it happened. I do respect the old stories. I don't say they're not true. I asked around the station to inquire from other people. One possible explanation was the trail or path from the Pali to the ocean that cuts through Wylie Station as straight as a die. It seemed to have something to do with these kinds of experiences whether it's attributed to Night Marchers or whatever.

After that I was transferred to another station. I do believe that there is a Supreme Being and that he is protecting me. Good thing!

Kakaako Station (Downtown Honolulu)

Fire Chief Cupid Joseph retired from the Hawaii State Fire Department and lived in Waimanalo with his family for many years. Chief Joseph shared the following stories during several interviews.

Shadow Man

During the 1850s when the Hawaii Fire Department really started, each ethnic group had their own station: Chinatown had a station and Pahoa down King Street was the Hawaiian station, mostly old Hawaiians living there. Some of these areas where the original stations are located are over a hundred years old. My dad was a fireman too. He was stationed at the old Palama station back in 1919. They had many incidents there. They had a "black man," a shadow man who used to attack a guy named Johnson. His last name was Ing, but his first name was Johnson and that's what we called him. Funny you hear that name, Johnson, and you run straight into a Chinese! Anyway, he was always the one bothered and he was the only one in the station ever bothered. He would see the guy too, although nobody else could see him.

The other stations that have "happenings" are Wylie, Kihipai, Kakaako, Kalihi, and Kaimuki. I was at the old station at Kakaako for years. Then I floated around in training and I've been here at Fireboat just over a year. I had a little dog. His name was Jingaling and he used to stand watch with me at night. The watch would start at 9 to 12, from 12 to 3 and 3 to 6 in the morning. We used to stand the first watch about midnight, and that's when it starts happening.

Now the kitchen of the old station was a separate building with a metal link fence. One night this guy and I went to get something

Old Kakaako Fire Station in downtown Honolulu.

to eat and we had to walk across and it's dark. All of a sudden he says, "You hear that?" Sure enough, there was this noise coming from the main dining room like somebody's there.

I said, "Oh, it's just my friend. Listen and you'll hear something start dragging."

Sure enough, we heard the sound of a heavy bench with metal legs start dragging across the floor with a screeetch, screeetch. (We had a heavy homemade bench in the dining room.) "Hey, somebody's doing that!" he said.

"Hey, nobody's doing that," I replied. We walked into the place and turned on the lights.

"Whoooooey!" says the guy. "There's nobody here!"

"Come now," I said. "Since he's around, I'm going to show you something else."

We turned the lights off and went into the office.

"Listen," I said. "Now you're gonna hear a primary bell. It goes ding, ding, ding, and before you can get a clear sound, you have to put a definite pressure on it. You might say that the timing has to be just right for the bell to go off. You're not going to set off the electrical bell. This is just a primary ding, ding, ding."

I took him into the apparatus room where the engines are and you could hear the song continue, ding, ding, ding. It kept right on. I don't know what it was or what was causing it, but it would come around regularly. It was just there. It was around the whole thirteen years I was at the old Kakaako Station.

Then there was Shadow Man. The first time I saw him we were all sitting around on the bench outside because of all the termites flying around the lights. It was about 11:30 at night. We all saw him: a guy walking from the garage area into the kitchen… or more like the shape of a guy walking. It was all black like a shadow or a silhouette.

"Hey!" I said. "Did you see it go into the kitchen?"

"Yeah, yeah."

"Did you see it come out?"

"No."

So we all went into the kitchen and it wasn't there. Nobody was there. We had a Dalmatian who used to ride the fire engines and he became our mascot. Generally, if a dog senses somebody around he growls. This particular dog used to whine at night, always at night, when we would see these figures. Usually when a dog senses somebody around, you can see the person. Not at old Kakaako!

There were so many instances of Chokeneck. There was one Lt. Yamoto, who was sleeping on the opposite side of me, and one night he started screaming and choking. Who was choking him I don't know, but he had fingerprint marks on his throat. When he moved out and someone else slept in that same bed, they got choked too. I thought it was real funny until one night, I was in my own bed and all of a sudden, somebody kicked me from under the mattress. Wham! One kick, you know, and I thought somebody was getting smart, so I did one somersault underneath the bed and started swinging. Nobody there. Not a soul. Couple of times, I woke up and somebody was holding me down, pushing on my chest and holding my arms. I looked up and I could see nothing. I say "Maki me, no way!" but I cannot move my head. It lasts maybe a few minutes. Then it goes away all of a sudden. My first impression is to look around thinking somebody is on top of me. I'm not saying it's the same "person" doing it. Might be a number of "persons."

Other people around there had that experience. Some people are superstitious and they used to stick *ti* leaves around and under their beds. I used to do that myself and here I was the top of the department sticking a *ti* leaf under my pillow! Oh well, everybody else was doing it. I figured there might be something to it. The one guy who was *always* getting choked was Bobby Loo. He used to sleep in there about four beds across from me.

One night he yells at me, "Do you see? Do you see the guy? He's walking out the door! Get me down off this bed and I'll stick my suitcase in his rear!"

"Well..." I said.

I went over to look at him and he was getting choked all right, the whole works. He was the only guy I knew who could see the figure. Nobody else could see him but Bobby. Another guy came up just then and said, "Is he having nightmares? Shall I wake him up?"

"No, no, no," I said, "Leave him alone. I think he's winning the fight. Don't bother him. If he's losing, wake him up. Otherwise, leave him alone."

Everybody started calling the Chokeneck, "Black Man." Hey, there's the Black Man!

Everyone knows that he's talking about some kind of spirit personality.

The Blessing of the Crooked Wall

The strip where Kakaako Fire Station is located was once a dump and a graveyard. This strip was known as the south side of town. You can see right across the street that they still have Kawaiahao Cemetery. All of central Honolulu was an ancient Hawaiian burial ground and even the tombstones go back to the 1880s.

I was here when they ripped down the old station shop and put up the new one. They were going to renovate, incorporate, enlarge and in the process had to put up a wall in back next to the roadway. So they were digging it all up and putting in the wall and it looked fine. The next morning, the men came to work and the wall was all *kapakahi* (crazy, all mixed up), all crooked out to here! The boss took one look and really chewed the guys out. Auweeee, no way! We know how to build walls and no way we going make a wall crooked like this."

The next day when they came in they couldn't believe what they saw. The wall was all crooked again and going every which way. The men said, "Aw, the firemen fooling with us." So they made everything straight once more. The next morning, they all came back and same thing. The wall all kapakahi every which way!

By this time one of the workers had dug up a skull and some bones. He went to the captain and said, "I think it will be to your benefit to go up to your church, be it Buddhist or whatever, or to Kawaiahao Church, and ask the minister to come bless this place."

He did take that advice. He went and got the assistant minister of Kawaiahao, Kapo, Reverend Akaka's assistant, to come to the site and bless it.

Reverend Kapo walked alongside the wall and when he came to one spot he stopped and said, "I want you to dig right here."

Sure enough, they unearthed a body and the wall went right across it. I guess he knew the history of the place and that area was known to be part of the graveyard.

They began to excavate and found a lot of skulls and bones. Kapo had them then dig one big hole and had them put all of the remains inside. I can relate what came next. He went to the hole and started to pray. He prayed and prayed in Hawaiian. All of a sudden he stopped praying and loudly said, "Shit! You had your day! Don't bother us anymore!"

And those are the exact words he used.

Well, Bishop Museum got wind of the thing and they came and wanted to look. One guy goes down into the hole with his little brush and started to brush the bones. He was trying to guess the age of that particular person. Then he wanted to take the bones out of there and remove the whole stuff for study. Kapo told him, "No, don't touch these bones! Leave everything just as it is and cover the grave." The guy started to insist that he wanted to take the bones, but Kapo told him in no uncertain terms to get out of the hole and he had to give it up. They gave the bones one final blessing after reburying them. The next morning, everything was okay.

The old station was next used for the Honolulu City Ballet!

The Pig Stealer

I'm not scared of spirits. I know what they are and I don't bother them. A cousin of mine once asked me to go hunting on Maui. We went out about five in the afternoon all around that mountain and we find nothing. I said, "If I was you, I would shoot the dog, poor thing. He couldn't find his way out of a sardine can!"

I left and went back to Hana. I could see my cousin take his dog back up into the mountain and I found out later that he caught two pigs.

I got one telephone call from him to tell me to come over and clean the two pigs. Uh oh, two pigs, I said, okay so back I went. We skinned the pigs, cut everything up to prepare to smoke the pork the next morning. He got ready to go home and put his pork in his car.

"Hey, what you doing?" I said. "You can't carry this stuff in the car. You'll get stopped."

"Rubbish!" he said. "I don't believe this 'pork over the Pali' rubbish."

"Hey," I warned, "You cannot fool around with this kind of stuff."

But he wouldn't pay any attention, so we got in the jeep and started out. Now this is 1 o'clock in the morning, right? All of a sudden, the lights go out and the car is kaput, completely dead. (Some of us says, "I think this is it!")

I got on top of the hood and my cousin, the skeptic, yells, "Hey, throw 'em"! Just geev'em!" But I said, "Hey, I'm telling you now I'm gonna eat off of this before I give you one piece!"

Just then another car came up the road and as soon as their lights hit our jeep, the engine started and the lights came back on.

I had learned not to fear. The first time this happened to me was when I got back from the service in Korea. I got a job hauling fish. We used to drive to Hilo in the middle of the night to deliver the fish, so I was driving in the dark a lot. One night I was driving with a guy from Kona who was quite experienced. We had just reached the Halfway House in Volcano as you go up to Kohala when there was a knock on the roof.

My relief driver was sleeping in back of the truck and had told me before we left that he would knock if he needed me. When I heard the knocks, I pulled over to the side of the road and yelled, "Yeah, what?"

He got out, looked around, and says, "Hey, where we at? What happened?"

"You're the one who's knocking," I said, but he replied that no, he never knocked.

I was mumbling what's the big idea, but when I went to start the engine there was nothing. Everything dead.

"Eh," I said, "throw some fish.

"Oh no! Don't throw nothing. I'll explain later."

Then he went *shishi* (urinated) around the wheels of the car! The lights came back on and the car started.

"Let's get outta here!" I yelled and after we got rolling I asked him to explain why you don't give.

186

"Once you give," he said, "you cannot start the car. You are stuck...*maka*! They will always stop the car I'm told, so you never give anything!"

I know there are happenings and I've seen them, but once you know where the power is coming from, you're not afraid—if you know what it is. The Maui incident was the last one for me. I've never had anything else happen for the past twenty years. I don't think there are any more or less incidents then there were twenty years ago. The same spirits that were bugging people then are bothering different people now! And more people have died in the last twenty years, so now it's their chance to start bothering people if they want to. Plus there's a whole bunch of angels got kicked out of Heaven so they could be caught up in this too. This stuff is still hanging around!

The Face on the Wall

I got a little granddaughter who was two and a half years old when this happened. She loved to sleep with us and one night she woke me up at one in the morning. My grandbaby says, "Poppa! Poppa! Looka da man over dere, Poppa. Poppa, get up!"

I thought she wanted her bottle, but she was pointing up to the corner of the room

"Yes, Baby. What man? Where the man?" I said.

"Dere, Poppa! Over dere on da wall. Look da man. He's coming down, he's coming down, he's coming down!" She was all excited. "Poppa, look dat! Coming down!"

Now I'm looking and I don't see anything, so I said, "What's he doing?"

"Oh, he's just looking. He's right dere in front of us."

So I'm looking and I don't see anything, but I got out of bed and turned on the lights. There was nothing, so I turned the light off and started to climb back in bed but my little grandbaby, she says, "Poppa, put the light back on. Turn it on!"

Oh, she's a smart one that one. Talk about Portuguese!

So I forgot about the incident. But a couple of days later, my wife was putting up a photograph on the wall of her mother and father. When my grandbaby saw it, she cried, "Oh Poppa! Look dat man. Dat's the man!"

Now what does she know! He had died long before she was born, but she pointed right at him and said, "Poppa, dat's the man."

My father-in-law had come to her. She is six years old now and every time something goes wrong or she seems to be in danger, he appears to her. It has happened half a dozen times now. It appears to be a warning.

One day she saw him just before she swallowed something and choked on it. She was spitting up green and we were all running around like a chicken without its head going crazy and then she was all right. Another time, she saw him just before she slipped off the balcony from the fourth floor of the apartment where we were living in Kailua. She went right on over. She fell on the canvas of the awning by the pool down below and just missed the metal knob on top. My oldest boy was the first one down after her and she was screaming bloody murder, not for her Momma but for me, her Poppa. Several times it seemed we were supposed to give her up, but before these things would happen, my wife's dad would show himself to her and she would be safe.

My wife always used to take her and her twin brother down to the graveyard to go "see" her parents. They loved to play on the lawn and pick flowers. She still likes to do that, to go down and "play with her grandfather." We believe he is watching over her and protecting her. He is her *aumakua.*

Menehune Walk

We used to see the Menehune walk. It was down in Punaluu. Back then you could see the riverbed, the stream that comes back down from the mountains to the ocean. On a certain night, they would walk right past the bedroom in back of our Aunt Jerry's house and you could actually see them. They were little people—Menehune—marching, walking. Small little people and a lot of them.

One night Aunt Jerry invited my dad and Chung (who stayed with my dad) out to see the Menehune walk. Oh, I was too late to go that night but I wish I had seen it! They went and they saw, but after awhile it got monotonous just watching little people walk. When they left the place, they were still walking. It is their pathway. Kaneohe is famous for that too.

The Ghost Who Threw Stones

One night my friends and I went fishing down at Mokuleia. We parked our car by the stone crusher there and we made camp. We walked to the place where we were going to fish and it was a long walk that night. We figured after a walk like that we'd be fishing all night but then we caught the fish. Lots and lots of mullet. We had them trapped inside our nets, so we said, 'Enough already, let's go home.' But this one friend, he said nooooo. We have to make one more catch, one for the river. I said okay, but what if we did make one more big catch? Who is going to carry all that stuff back? I like mullet too, but there are only three of us so who's going to carry?

But no, no we have to so I said alright. I caught one fish, a small one, and I threw him back in the water. Then we got some seaweed in the net. Then comes one rock thrown at my friend. Hey, he says, who threw the rock? Nobody threw a rock, I said. But he replied, oh yeah? Look up on the beach and see that guy standing there!

So I looked up on the beach and I do see a guy standing there. I said that's who threw the rock. I'll go talk to him. So I went up on the beach at Mokuleia, all the way up, and I was walking towards him and he was backing up. I ran up on the sand to look for him and wow! Nobody there... He couldn't have disappeared like that. There was no place to go.

Now I know my two friends. They're scared of ghosts. So when I joined them back in the ocean, I said, aw, he had to go. I didn't want to scare them, you see.

We picked up our nets again and one said, hey looka da guy. There he is again. I said oh, yeah. We picked up the nets and everything to go home. I was carrying the nets and the others were carrying the fish. Then we heard the guy call, yoooo hooooo, like somebody hardly calling, but more like breathing on your ear. And I'm telling my friends don't run, don't run, don't run. Take your time. And then the rocks came flying!

Rocks begin to fly, but never hit us; always missed us and never harmed us. And there is this singing—whooo, whoooo—singing, calling, rocks flying! Then there was a whistle, a sharp whistle, and the figure on the beach started to sing! And it was the most beautiful thing I ever heard in my life that music. Singing! The words didn't make sense, but the music... No instruments, just singing, beautiful singing.

It was the one night of the month the Hawaiians call Pokani, the night of the spirits roaming. It has to do with the moon, the darkest part of the moon. It was supposed to be a good night to fish, the best fishing, but it's not a good night to fish. The spirits are out!

Kahuna 'Ana 'Ana

This is a true story. Sometimes it's a little hard to believe, but they have proof that these things took place.

My grandfather was a representative from Maui and a good friend of Prince Kuhio. Just before my grandmother was due to give birth, it became apparent she was going to have twins. Another friend of my grandfather, a man named McBride from Kauai, asked if he could *hanai* in the Hawaiian way and have one of the babies to raise as his own. My grandfather agreed and McBride was given the first son to be born. The first baby to come was David and the second boy was my father, Cupid. It was truly a "here-he-is, he's-yours" kind of thing in the old Hawaiian tradition. So David went to Kauai and my dad stayed on Maui.

Now it seemed that there was a grand uncle of ours who was supposed to be one of the greatest *kahuna* from Maui. He was descended from the Kamehameha line of *kahunas.* His father and his father's father were all *kahunas* and had passed their lore right down the line. Luckily this uncle was the last in the line. He died in the 1920s and he never had a family so he didn't pass it on to anyone. Thank goodness! This relative was a master of black *huna* or 'ana'ana. He possessed tremendous power and could foretell the future and even kill people. And he did kill people... anyone who crossed him in any way.

Everyone was afraid of him and there are many stories about him. He was so strict that he was unyielding and he was also very jealous.

One day he came to my grandmother with a chilling message: the baby on Kauai was going to die. My grandmother broke down.

"Why?" she sobbed. "Why?"

This uncle was jealous that a man named McBride had taken one of the babies to another island to raise as his own. My grandmother was frantic and pleaded with the uncle to save the child. She wanted to do something—anything—to save the baby.

"Watch out!" warned the uncle, "Or the other one will die too!"

"Oh my God!" My grandmother wailed as she didn't want to lose my father as well. She pleaded so hard that the old man finally instructed her to come to his house that night and made her promise to do exactly as he told her.

When she did appear, he gave her a sweet-smelling leaf and told her to walk as far as she could while smelling it. When you are tired, he said, you are to stoop and mark the place right there. Keep smelling the leaf and hold it to your nose. Then go back home. The next night, repeat the same thing again.

She did as she was told in an effort to save her baby. She reported that she sensed "something" like an obstacle in front of her all the way trying to block her. She went all the way smelling the leaf and marked the spot. When she returned, the uncle was waiting for her. He gave her a rock and told her to step into the house, but before crossing through the door she was to throw the rock hard behind her. My grandmother did as she was told.

The next morning the old man came to her saying, "*Make, make, the baby is dead and so is the man who took him. He died too.*"

My grandmother was heartbroken and she had to wait for two weeks before she got the news that the baby had indeed died and McBride had died too... crushed by a boulder! (Remember, this was back in 1901 and the communication in those days was very slow. It took days and even weeks to get word from one island to another.) You see what she had to do was symbolic of what was going to happen. Both the baby and the man had been crushed by a boulder, but my father was safe. She had saved him.

It was no wonder that people were afraid of this uncle. Once someone stole a couple of pigs from him. He passed the word that whoever stole the pigs should come and tell him and nothing would happen to them. Nobody paid attention. Nobody came. So then he passed out the word that whoever took the pigs was going to die.

"They're gonna *make*!" he said, "They're gonna die, but before they do they're gonna squeal like pigs!"

The curse was thrown. Sure enough, three guys fell down on their hands and knees squealing like pigs, raising a terrible commotion before they died, one by one. Oh, he was something else, this uncle!

There was another incident, which helped to make this uncle infamous. It seems there was a well on his property for drinking water. Somebody took baby droppings and threw them in the water one day. Uncle passed the word again: whoever did that, come over and clean it up. Nobody came. He wasn't messing around this time either.

He said, "The baby who owns that dies!"

And sure enough, the baby died. Oh yeah, he didn't fool around.

The shack he lived in is still there today. It's just past Seven Pools on the top of a hill in a *kamani* grove. Nobody goes into that place. All of the shacks around have had their boards taken out for salvage and have been dismantled, but nobody touches his shack. If you have no business inside there, you'd better not go in.

He was a black sheep in our family. I'm not interested in tracing any of my family back there. Let them stay there.

The Bad Luck Lava Rock

Larry Almeida and the men of Kakaako Fire Station in downtown Honolulu contributed to this story.

This is a fairly new fire station here at Kakaako. I don't know when the original station was built, but I know they had horses

at one time. This whole area is spooky and you've got all these old places like the graveyard right across the street and the old Royal Brewery next door. There are a lot of stories connected with the old station, but we've just had a few things happen around the new one.

A couple of years ago we were all sitting around the kitchen when the telephone book moved across the table all by itself. Nobody touched it. Nobody was near it. That was weird. It's a heavy book and it literally flew off the counter by itself.

Then there was a garbage can that did the same thing and took off across the floor all by itself. Again no one was near it at all. Then we had one man who swore that he was pushed off the upstairs when he was the only guy up there. He was standing by the pole and all of a sudden he fell off. We don't know if he just fell by himself or what, but that was his excuse. Every time something inexplicable happens, we just blame it on "Kimo."

Some people sleep with *ti* leaves under their beds here. We did have two guys choked at this station. They were both captains and in the captain's room at the time. Actually, come to think of it, we've got quite a few guys here who got choked. One guy was lying on a big wooden chair outside taking a nap in broad daylight when he started getting choked. He clutched his throat and started shaking and making funny noises. Everybody laughed. They thought he was kidding, but no, he was really in trouble.

Sometimes you can hear the oil cans shaking and rattling under the fire truck when there is no wind and nobody around. Once in awhile, if it's very still, you can hear footsteps walking around upstairs when no one is there. Kimo gets around!

Nothing much happens to me. My *tutu* (grandmother) takes care of me, right? Russell Kim of #6 really caught it once though. He was on the Big Island where the volcano is and he brought back a lava rock from the crater itself. It was very nice looking really, but my god, he had to take it back! This is a true story. When I met him, I was working half time so I was able to meet him at the airport when he came back from the Big Island. He got off the plane carrying two big packages and I asked him what is that? Lava rocks, he said. You like one? Sure, give me one. Hey, nice. I saw the rock and it was really nice. Now, I am Hawaiian and I believe in those things, but I don't *really* believe, if you know what I mean. However, my parents and grandparents, they take it very seriously.

Anyway, I took that rock home and the first thing I did was call my mom to see if I should keep it. She asked me where it was from and I really didn't know where he had picked it up. She told me if he had gotten it away from the crater, that it was all right. I said that I thought he had gotten it right from the place where the craters were located near to the eruption. *Take it back!* said my mom.

Lava Rocks

In the meantime, Russell is down at the station on night duty. He was asleep when somebody starts pulling his toe and twisting it hard. He woke up and looked around and nobody there. As soon as he goes back to sleep, somebody starts twisting his toe all over again. This happened for three nights in a row.

I said to him, "Hey Larry, it's the rock. Take him back!"

By this time, I had given the other rock to a Hawaiian guy named Harry Kuakane. Russell is getting all scared now saying that he had to take *both* rocks back where they came from. Hey, I said, you gotta go look for Harry. Harry got 'em.

I don't know how he tracked Harry down, but he did it. He made a special trip to the Big Island to take both rocks back and after that everything was fine.

Makiki Station

The following conversation took place at old Makiki Station with Nappy Napoleon and Aaron Kikuchi one night in October 1984 as we sat on a stonewall and park benches underneath a mango tree beneath a full Halloween moon. It was a perfect setting for ghost stories.

Talk Story Under a Full Moon

Old Kakaako Station had all kinds of things. It was built on old *heiau* grounds.

Nappy Napoleon was a tall, big Hawaiian fireman. He stood with one foot on the park bench as he began to speak.

"Old Makiki Station is a sister station to the one in Kakaako and they were both built in the 1920s. They look alike and the one down on Kalihi Street is similar also. In fact, Kaimuki, Kakaako, and Kalihi Stations were all built in the same year and are under the Federal Historical society. The problems now are in maintenance of these stations. The ceilings are termite ridden, the beams are rotten, and the floors are cracking. It's too much money to restore and the timbers are too big inside to replace, but they're going to try their best to get the termites out."

"There is quite a bit of history here and these old stations all have their stories. This station—Makiki—was used as a morgue for several years back in the 1930s. They never had the morgue then like they have now down at Queens Hospital so they put the bodies in plastic bags and left them here overnight. The guys who used to stand watch downstairs said the scariest part was when the muscles would twitch and the bags would move. That really gives you a start! None of the guys liked to stand watch downstairs."

"Yeah," Nappy continued with a faraway expression, "this was kind of a spooky station. The fire truck was used as a hearse and we had to take all the equipment off. We don't have to do that anymore. Now they use the old museum truck down at Kalihi Station. They use it for parades too. Too much hassle otherwise.

"There was one man who died upstairs in his sleep. Nobody ever knew exactly what killed him. Maybe a heart attack. Maybe he had Chokeneck and couldn't take it. Nobody knows..."

"Chokeneck happened to me about twelve years ago," Aaron Kikuchi broke in. "I was stationed here, I moved to another station and then I came back. I couldn't see anything when it got me. I was looking for something I could get a fix on, but I couldn't see anybody. I kept a lamp burning on the floor after that. There already were *ti* leaves in the bed."

He paused before continuing.

"For about a year I stayed up all night. I mean it. I stayed up every night for one year and I went home and slept during the day. One year. The funny thing is that when this happened, I had a friend standing right by me and he didn't even hear me. Another guy, Doug, was sleeping a couple of beds away and he didn't hear. I felt like I was yelling, yeah! I saw him stand up and after it was over I asked if he had heard me yelling. He said no."

"I never had anything like that happen to me before. When I was a kid growing up, I used to have a reoccurring dream. I would moan and my mom would wake me up, but that was nothing like this. I saw ocean waves—lots of waves—and then I saw a picture in my mind of a beach with some marines in full pack and gear, war pack, running up the beach with a palm leaf swaying in front of them. Then I didn't have any other dreams after that. Every once in a while I feel like that thing is coming on and I would think of the marines on the beach and that would wipe it out. But that was nothing like Chokeneck. When that happens, your whole body is paralyzed. I tried my best to move or turn over and I couldn't! There is this feeling of pressure on your chest that goes along with it. They call it 'Chokeneck' and that's as good a name as any. When you know you're going to Makiki Station, people say 'oh, Chokeneck!' Word gets around."

Nappy sat down on the bench and rested his elbows on his knees. He cleared his throat and said, "That hasn't happened to me at Makiki, but we had a time once at Kakaako Fire Station. We had an alarm that day. It was about two o'clock in the afternoon and most of the guys were asleep. (We always sleep.) The alarm came and the guy next to me was lying flat on his back, looking straight up at me. He says, 'I cannot get up, Nappy! This guy is sitting on my chest!' He's struggling to get up and he cannot. He could feel something pressing down on his chest and he just cannot get up. He's asking me for help and I say, 'I ain't helping you. That guy's gonna jump on me!" At first I thought he was joking, then I see that he really cannot get up. So I slid down the pole and told the captain to go 'cause this guy ain't coming."

"After all what are good friends for, yeah? And the funny part is this guy's the state karate champion! Of course he missed the truck and had to buy us ice cream and cake. We didn't wait. We couldn't and when we came back, he was okay. Kind of mad though."

"Down there, Captain Bobby Loo got choked every single night. This was back in the 1960s. Well, nothing happened to me so I got curious and attempted to see the ghost...if that's what it was. I went to sleep in the early afternoon, but before I did I said, 'Hey, I want to see you! I want to see what you look like. Come on out!' An invitation to a ghost, so to speak. Well, he did! And I got scared. You know when you're sleeping it's so warm and all of a sudden it's *cold, cold, cold* just like ice.

"Now I've been cold, but not this cold, not like ice. I was so scared I couldn't even open my eyes. I'm not Catholic, but I said the Hail Mary Full of Grace twenty times and I said the Lord's Prayer twenty-five times. When the thing finally went away and I got warm again, I slid down the pole and the first thing I did was call my father who is an assistant minister for our church. Of course he gave me a good scolding and told me not to play around with this stuff. He said I could get hurt messing around with this. For about a month after that I never went to sleep unless somebody else was up there too. When they went downstairs, I went downstairs too!"

"I never saw the guy because I couldn't open my eyes, but Bobby Loo used to see the guy coming towards him and he was sleeping only four feet away from me. 'Ooooooooooh,' he used to yell, 'it's coming, it's coming! Look at those red feet!' Well, I'm looking and I don't see anything. Then he goes, 'Aghhhhhhhh!' and he's getting choked. This guy is getting choked every single night and he's sticking ti leaves in every four corners of his mattress, in his pillowcase, everywhere. Every single night he gets choked at just about the same time, between one and two o'clock in the morning. After a while, we don't even think about it since he's the only one who can see it. The rest of us just turn over and go to sleep. I did try to stay up nights to see it, but I cannot, so I asked my father what he thought was happening. He thought that someone had a bad grudge against him or he's got something in him that brings this thing back and back and back. This Bobby Loo was one tough Chinese guy too. He used to box and he knew kung fu, but when this guy with the red feet came, there wasn't much he could do. He finally moved stations and went to Palolo. Then he retired."

Nappy took a deep breath and let it out between his teeth with a hissing noise.

"Sheeeeeesh. Firemen are a pretty tough bunch and this Bobby Loo...he could handle anybody. And I mean anybody! But when something like this grabs you, well… what are you going to do? It's one thing to hear it happening to other guys. They tell you and you don't want to believe it. But when it happens to you, I tell you, that's something else again. When that brother with the red feet comes, I don't care how tough you are, you collapse!"

Makoana Station

Gerald Brown was Captain of Makoana Station on Maui and a part-time cowboy. He has experienced repeated attacks of "Chokeneck."

The Ghost Upstairs

I've been a fireman for twenty years. I was only twenty-four years old when I was transferred to Makiki Station. Nobody told me about "Chokeneck" and being a probie (on probation) you kind of keep to yourself. Everyone was already assigned their bed when I arrived and there was one open bed so I took it. It was okay for a couple of months. Then it started to happen.

Usually it would come right after dark or just before daylight. It's a heavy sensation of being pressed down on the bed and you are choking, but you are conscious. You know what I mean? If people are talking, you know what they are saying. If the television is on, you can watch the program. Meanwhile, you're going through this mean trauma!

Well, it would come and it would go and I thought that maybe there was really something wrong with me. As I was only twenty-four, I ruled out cardiac arrest. I didn't want to tell anybody. Finally maybe six months had gone by.

I had a driver named Benny Aquillo. He was wrapped up in the Massey murder case back in 1936. Anyway when I was on watch and Benny would go upstairs to answer the phone, I noticed that he always carried some *ti* leaves. One day I asked him what he was doing it for and he began to tell me stories of one Chokeneck upstairs. When I said that I also had that problem, he advised me to take one *ti* leaf too. He explained that I was sleeping right in the path of whatever it was.

By this time it had happened so often that I could actually see it coming and I had learned to throw myself off of the bed before it reached me. It would form by the window and float directly across the room over to my bed. It was like cigarette smoke until it reached the bed and then it would begin to take a shape. There were streetlights outside so it was never dark within the dorm. It would come from the far side of the window on the second story. There were beds along three walls shaped like big U. I was in the corner while in the middle was a ping-pong table. People on watch in the office downstairs used to get it too in the location right under my bed, but nowhere else in the station. There was a watch called The Honolulu Code and somebody had to be on it at all times. Watches went from nine to twelve and the next guy would wake up and go from one to four. Then the next guy would report at seven-thirty. There was always somebody awake, but we used to cheat and we would sleep. That's when people would get Chokeneck.

It would happen like four or five times in a row, but it would be months in-between times. It always happened however when the moon was like a horseshoe in the last quarter. I started taking a ti leaf to bed with me and it stopped coming. After a while I had it wired and I would watch for the last quarter of the moon and take *ti* leaves to bed. Funny thing. When I first put my linen on this bed, I turned my mattress over and there were dried *ti* leaves between the two mattresses. Until Benny told me what they were for I never knew even though I am part-Hawaiian. Benny also told me if I would curse or spit or jump up and down when I saw this thing coming it would pass me by. After I learned to throw myself off the bed I was able to avoid it. Otherwise there you would be with this thing on top of you—this big mass of something—where you can't breathe, you can't fight, and you think you're screaming when you're not making a sound. It's like you're literally fighting, but you're not moving at all while you have this huge weight on your chest pressing you down into the mattress. It's like you're coming up from the depths and you're running out of air. After it passes, you're all covered with sweat from fighting this imaginary—**BUT VERY REAL**—thing, you're gasping and you're wide awake!

It seemed like it lasted for hours, but it was probably only seconds. My friend had a television and he slept across from me. A lot of times I would just be lying there watching TV, dozing off, and it would happen; yet I never missed anything on the program. I knew what was going on the whole time. I used to be embarrassed because in my opinion it was a nightmare, right?

It never happened late at night, always early, maybe ten or eleven or perhaps four or five in the morning. Never at midnight. A lot of times the other guys would be talking and laughing and this would happen. It's pretty heavy on the brain, you know.

There were three of us at Makiki who had this happen all the time. I think a lot of guys have it, but don't talk about it for fear people would laugh or say they were dreaming. It only happened to me in Honolulu and I believe I was the only one who saw it coming. Maybe some other people have, but they just won't talk about it. Sometimes there was a head, sometimes just smoke, sometimes just a form. I told my mom about it. My dad was very Hawaiian, but it's not something you go around broadcasting, is it?

I never did find out what caused it. At first I thought it was the inhalation of all the smoke I got on the job. I knew it wasn't cigarette smoke because nobody on my side of the room smoked. It happened to me so often and I got so adept at throwing myself off of the bed that I was always waking everybody up and nobody wanted me around. I had a real reputation for falling off the bed!

Although I had never heard of such a thing as Chokeneck before I went to Makiki Station I had heard that the station itself was haunted. Towards the end of my tour we moved the beds around upstairs and it seemed to stop. Then I was told that maybe it was a path where the warriors or Night Marchers would come, as the old people used to say. I haven't been back to Makiki since I left. I was glad when they transferred me out of there.

Nothing has happened to me here on Maui. I'm a cowboy part-time and we go out on roundup every three months. We

203

have 36,000 acres to cover on the leeward side of the island and up around Seven Pools. There's nothing there for miles and miles, no people, nothing. You don't run across anybody and that's where we come across all kinds of artifacts, house sites, lava tubes, caves, and calabashes... Once we found a canoe in a cave in the mountains almost two miles from the sea. It was damp, but I guess it was dry enough to preserve it. We don't know why it was there; it was so far from the sea. Normally that would be a burial cave. It was so deep, it went on and on back into the mountain, but there were no bones, just seashells. The canoe was just beginning to deteriorate.

I do things like this for a pastime and nothing has ever happened to me. I haven't even stubbed my toe! One time though it happened to a friend of mine. This was a *haole* family. They live up in Ilima now. I found this cave with a lot of artifacts, calabashes, and stuff like that. He was curious to see it so I drew him a map, but I warned him to leave it alone as it was a burial cave.

About three months later he came to my house and was he upset! He had a box with him and said, "We've got to take this back!"

"Take what back?" I said.

He opened the box and I recognized what I had seen in the cave except the calabashes were starting to crack. He told me that his house had burned down, his horse had hung on his rope, his baby had gotten sick, and he'd been in a traffic accident, all in a matter of weeks. It was five in the afternoon and getting dark. It was twenty miles to the lava tubes, but he insisted on going to return the stuff right then. So we dashed out of there, found the cave and went in. There were skeletons all over the place—one whole skeleton was sitting up—and we put everything back where it belonged and got out of there. He was okay after that. Outside of that one incident, I never got scared; I never took anything from a cave and nothing ever happened to me. Only at Makiki Station, but that was enough!

Fireboat Station, Honolulu Harbor

A large, strong Hawaiian man from Maui, Gabriel "Abner" Hinau, was stationed at both Wylie in Nuuanu and Fireboat in Honolulu Harbor.

(Author's note: After I left Hawaii and moved to Oregon, I had occasion to contact Gabriel, although it had been over a year since we had communicated. I searched everywhere for his telephone number and address, but to no avail. He was unlisted so I couldn't call the operator. I decided the information must have been lost in the move and was forced to give up. Within the hour, the telephone rang. It was Gabriel! "There's something?" he said.)

Aulele

When I was a boy growing up in Maui, all kinds of things happened to me. I often went diving. Back then when a man drowned, a Japanese priest would tear up red paper into little bits and throw the pieces into the water in the belief that a piece would sink to the bottom and find the drowned man. They would then dive over and find the body. They believed in this as a kind of law of attraction. Well, one day I went diving for fish and I felt myself being attracted to the side of a cove where I had never been before. I felt a strong desire to climb up the right side of the lava rock cliff so while my friend fished, that's exactly what I did. I found a wonderful cave filled with skulls and bones. I seemed to have my own law of attraction.

Another time I had gone turtle hunting with a friend and his father who carried a carbine in his car. He would spot the turtles from the top of a cliff and shoot them in the head. Then my friend and I would have to dive thirty or forty feet from the cliff to fetch them. This time I was out in the water after a turtle when I had a strong desire to swim to a ledge and climb up onto it to rest.

I did and when I leaned back and put my hand into the sand, I grabbed a bunch of human hair. It was on a body buried just beneath the sand.

I learned early on not to talk about my experiences. My mother told me it was just "a bunch of trash" and not to pay any attention to it. I was raised in both the Christian and the old Hawaiian ways. However these kinds of experiences kept happening to me.

When I was young, I used to hear music outside of Lahaina town where we lived: slack key guitar music and sometimes whistling, a good tune, like someone could whistle really well. It was pretty and I liked to listen to it. One day I decided to watch it too. I followed the sound to the *Vi Vee* apple tree in the corner of our yard and looked through the branches expecting to see who was making the music. No one was there.

When I was a teenager, I was with both my parents on the lanai in Maui one afternoon. I looked up and saw this *aulele* or fireball about the size of a balloon with a tail trailing three or four feet behind. It was about five hundred feet away from us at rooftop height. It was bright orange with a yellow tail like a comet and it was traveling horizontally very slowly. Then it exploded and disappeared. My parents didn't say anything. They knew about these things. They had seen these things before. They just turned around and went into the house.

The Headless Woman

There are so many stories, but I try not to think of them. I want to forget. I have been told that I have psychic ability, but I want to leave it alone. I don't want to stir it up, you know.

One day a lady friend of mine asked if I would help her find out if a girlfriend of hers was okay. She hadn't heard from her in a long time and was worried, as she was unable to locate her. I had known her before myself, but still she gave me four snapshots of her. That night before I went to bed I looked at the photos and concentrated on the girl. I fell asleep and woke up all of a sudden. I thought perhaps it was just a vivid dream, but I saw a figure standing at the foot of my bed slightly off to one side.

Suddenly the figure jumped in bed with me and was lying against my back. I thought to myself, "I'm a big strong man. I can turn over and take care of this." I looked over my shoulder and saw a woman in blue slacks and a blue silk shirt with sleeves to her wrists...but no head! The next day I saw my lady friend and told her, "I don't know where your friend is, but don't look for her. She isn't on the planet anymore." Three months later, her body was discovered buried in Alaska. She had been decapitated.

When I was stationed at Nuuanu, lots of guys would have trouble sleeping and would make gurgling noises. They wouldn't like to talk about it because the other guys might make fun. We called it "Chokeneck." More than once I was choked so I knew what it was like. Now I like to work out a lot, lift weights, jog, and all of that so I was in good shape, but when this thing would happen you couldn't move! It was like a pressure weighing you down. You were paralyzed and your eyes were open, but there was nothing there. Then it would go away and you would be so weak afterwards, so tired. Usually I can jump right out of bed in the dark when we get a fire call and for a few seconds it's like there's a light on and you can see everything automatically, jump into your boots and the next thing you know, you're flying down the street on the truck. But when Chokeneck happens, you can't move.

One time I was asleep when suddenly I opened my eyes and saw this thing moving towards me. It was shaped like a snake with a head and an eye, but no mouth. It slowly wiggled towards me and I yelled a few four-letter words at it and it disappeared. Just like that. But then that feeling came and I couldn't move.

About a year later I was visiting my buddy and his new wife in their apartment. His wife was in the kitchen fixing *pupus* (snacks) and stuff. We had been having a drink and talking when my eye fell on this picture on the wall. The wife came out of the kitchen just then and I asked her where the picture came from. It was here when we moved in, she said. It was an original painting on bamboo. There was bamboo in the background and coming out of the bamboo was the same thing I had seen in my bed a year before—black, snake-like, about six inches long. I told her to get rid of it, as it was evil and a thing of witchcraft. She broke it up and put it in the trashcan. I didn't even want to touch it with my hands. One encounter was enough!

Premonition of a Disaster

Sometimes I sense things. Once I worked part-time for Shell Oil Company. It was a good job and I could work anytime I wanted. I was retained to train the employees for safety. They had just passed the hundred thousand day mark without an accident. Now that's a perfect record, so I had gone out with a buddy that Friday night to celebrate. He was divorced and had two little kids. We had a drink or two in the bar across the street from the station and my friend said, "You know, if anything happens to me I just want my two kids taken care of. Just do right by my two kids, will you?" He went on to say, "I know a lot of women, but I just feel as if I'm way up here and they are all way down there." I gave him my interpretation of that and told him that he couldn't form a bond with any of them because he felt like he was above them all playing around in Heaven.

Three times that night he brought up the same conversation and we started talking about catastrophes and what might happen. We moved to a second bar where a lot of Hawaiian guys hang out and again the conversation centered around catastrophes and calamities. We moved to Eddies and talked more of the same. The next morning was the Shell explosion. My friend was on duty along with another guy I knew. They were in the first flash explosion and they got burned. The one they sent to the burn clinic in Texas, he lived thirteen days. My friend was sent to St. Francis in San Francisco and he lingered a long time. I sent him a recovery card even though I knew he probably couldn't see it. Flash fires burn the tissue and blind. But I sent him the card anyway in both English and Hawaiian. I wrote, "Look, I want you to get well, but if you don't have any reason to stay on, go. Go straight to God. You're free." He went soon after. When you have burns over fifty percent of your body, it's hard to get well.

A short time after that I had a dream. It was a sharp vivid dream and I remembered it. I dreamt that my friend had come back to Shell and was standing by the pole in the main room. That day I heard that Reverend Akaka had come to Shell to bless it. I wasn't there to see it, but I asked where he had stood. They pointed to the exact spot I had seen my friend stand when he had come back in my dream the night before.

I don't like to talk about this, but I had another dream a couple of weeks before the fire. I dreamt that I was at the airport watching a plane land, a DC3 taxi in. Then I was close to the plane and I saw a doorway open and a forklift brought down a closed coffin. It was so clear. Later when I went to my friend's funeral (how often do you go to a funeral?) I looked down at his coffin and it was the same coffin as the one I had seen in my dream. Exactly.

4

What IS a Ghost?

A Spirited Conversation with Charles Kenn

On November 17, 1986, I met with Charles Kenn at a coffee shop in Kaneohe, Oahu. He was a gentleman with silver hair, a quiet smile, and great dignity. We spent a fascinating hour and a half together as he generously shared his personal opinions, insights, and knowledge of Hawaiian spiritual lore gathered over a long lifetime in the Islands. Kenn was selected as a Living Treasure by the Honpa Hongwanji Mission of Hawaii. Julius S. Rodman stated, "I've known Charles Kenn about fifty years. I have unreserved aloha and respect for him. No doubt about it, Kenn is the supreme authority among Hawaii scholars." Sammy Amalu, columnist for the *Star Bulletin*, said, "The dear man has truly forgotten more about Hawaii than the rest of us will probably ever recall in our entire lifetime!" The following interview strongly expresses Mr. Kenn's personal opinions and does not in any way reflect the opinions of the author.

"**M**r. Kenn," I began, "what is your definition of a ghost?"

He thought for a moment before replying. I was unaware at that point that I was about to be the unique beneficiary of a powerful lecture on the subject.

"First of all," he said slowly, "point of view is most important. Mrs. Mary Kawena Pukui in her dictionary of Hawaiian words has many different shades of meaning for the word *lapu* and very many different words for "ghost." Now all these different words that Mrs. Pukui uses pertain to different experiences. Many of them, from my

210

Charles W. Kenn, scholar and kahuna, was selected as one of Hawaii's Living Treasures.

point of view, do not come under the true definition of "ghost," but this is the way she was taught. When people would ask her, "How come you know so much about this and so much about that?" she comes out with the statement, "That is the way I was taught."

So whenever we speak of our experiences or tell people about various things, it always comes from within our own experience or from what we were taught. There are conflicting or different points of view. Among the Hawaiians, you have probably experienced their differing points of view even to the point of argument or conflict, their getting "hot headed." You've probably heard of Max Freedom Long and his teachings. You've probably heard of Serge King and his group. They talk about what they call *huna*.

They each define *huna* in a certain way. Now I suppose that *huna* can be defined as a ghost or a certain kind of ghost, but that *huna* literally is "secret" or that which is secret or hidden from a person who has not had that particular experience. Now from the Hawaiian point of view it means not what is hidden, but that which is revealed. Just the opposite: to reveal! So in *huna* we have that which is hidden or kept secret and that which reveals at the same time like a dream. A dream can be like a ghost in a way.

Take two dictionaries, one in Hawaiian-English and the other in English-Hawaiian. When you look up the word "ghost" in the English-Hawaiian section, you are given different Hawaiian words. Yet when you look up these words that Mrs. Pukui reveals to you in Hawaiian,

Charles W. Kenn with master firewalkers from Huahini. Kenn is author of *Firewalking from the Inside. Courtesy of Firewalking from the Inside.*

you realize that it's her point of view she is presenting. If you went to any other Hawaiian and you used these words, they would say no, that is not correct.

For example, Mrs. Pukui would use the word *akua.* To some Hawaiians, *akua* has nothing to do with ghosts. Some people talk about the full moon as a ghost, but there are two meanings for the "full moon." I don't know if you have gone into the Hawaiian concept today of *po* and *au. Po* means night and *au* means day. But to the traditional Hawaiians, *po* refers to the time when to the Hawaiian mind civilization was ruled by women in a matrilineal form of family. It was not exactly a period of darkness, as we understand it today, but that time when the world was matrilineal. So when we have the ghost of *po,* it is one thing and when we have the ghost of *au,* which is today's world, it is another thing.

So you are dealing with a ghost of what the Hawaiians call *au,* which has come to mean "light." *Po* has come to mean "dark." We say *Po-o-kane* meaning the night of Kane. Now it does not necessarily mean that but rather the period when Kane held sway, a period before Captain Cook and the white man. When we say the *po* of Lono, the *po* of Ku and so forth, we don't mean the "night" of that particular person or god. The Hawaiians had no religion; they had no gods. The word *akua* does not mean "god" in the original Hawaiian. The word *akua* means *makua*, which means a father or a parent.

This brings in the concept I was mentioning to you of the *aumakua*—the *makua* of the *au.* And to the Hawaiian, the *au* is the permanent, the universal all-pervading spirit...a ghost that some Hawaiians refer to as the *kumulipo.*

The *kumulipo* has been misunderstood by Beckwith. I don't think she had any indication of what the word really means. What she did was to take an old translation by a Hawaiian man named David Kupelehea. He gave her his translation of that so-called "prayer," but here again, the Hawaiians did not pray so they had no word for prayer. The word *pule* means crazy, the root of the word *pupule.* Now when the Hawaiians say *pupule* they refer to a person who is flighty in the sense of being hazy or off the rocker. A person that is not all there we call *pulepule* and so the word *pupule* means crazy in that sense. When the missionaries used the word *pule* to mean prayer, therefore, it means when you pray you are crazy!

Hewahewa was the high priest of Kamehameha. Mrs. Pukui gives the word *hewahewa* as meaning crazy. Oliver Emerson, the son of the Reverend John Emerson (who used to be at Wailua) wrote a book called *Frontiers of Hawaii*. He knew Hewahewa personally and he had been told that during Kamehameha's time, Hewahewa would lead the army holding the figure of Kukanelopu in effigy while saying crazy things alluding to the fact that these crazy sayings were really coming from the effigy he was holding. A person who is crazy is living in another world or plane or dimension. That is the difference between that the Hawaiians refer to as *po* and *au*. *Po* not only refers to the coming of the missionaries but it is an example that the westerners had here in the Pacific—even before the time of Jesus.

There are so many viewpoints. There is a viewpoint by Max Freedom Long who has come to be like a god to many people. There is a group in Missouri run by a man named Reingold whom Max had appointed as his successor. There is a lot of material Max had written on *huna* there. From 1935 to the day he died in 1971, he wrote voluminous data on the subject, which has been compiled. People like Serge King have extracted from this data and have included Max and his material in their own viewpoint. To me they are following the ghost of Max as he followed the ghost of Dr. Brigham. Max was a student of Dr. Brigham from the Bishop Museum and speaks of him in his writings as being a prophet. Max writes of how Dr. Brigham told him of the reality of the supernatural as a power that exists but is not yet developed which the ordinary scientist is not yet in tune with. He spoke of being in tune with the world of ghosts. The supernatural collates ghosts from the point of view of the intellectual so that today's view of ghosts has to be almost anything to do with the supernatural. Yet when scientists today refer to the supernatural, the Hawaiian *kahuna* would say there is no such thing. The supernatural was natural to the *kahuna*. Ghosts were natural to the *kahuna*.

The Hawaiians had a word for people having visions: *akaku*. Aka is a shadow and *ku* is to stand. Then they had *no'o*, which is to sit, so they described both sitting and standing apparitions. Max split the word *kahuna* into *ka* and *huna*. In *huna* he refers to the hidden, the esoteric when actually there is no such thing just as there is no such thing as that which is hidden. If it is hidden from you it's all because you have a different point of view. The phrase, "Now you finally see the light" is when you talk to a person and he believes what you say because the dimension of that person's world or viewpoint is no different from your experience. He is looking at it from the same window, so to speak. If one is looking at an object from a different angle when your angle has to do with your own experience, then you do not agree.

One of the best books to read by Long is *Recovering the Ancient Magic* or *The Hidden Science Behind Miracles.* Both books will give you an idea of how Max came to his viewpoint of what the *kahunas* were like and what they were taught and you will get a picture of what these different people were thinking.

I can tell you a lot of stories about the *aumakua* point of view that occurred not only in my experience, but also in the experience of members of my family. These were experiences that came from within us and not as a result of outside forces. They come from our own subconscious. Max refers to the three selves of the *kahunas.* He calls the conscious mind *uhane*, the subconscious mind the *umipili,* and the higher conscious or super-conscious, the *amakua,* which is outside of man, outside of the world. Some people go on to say that *amakua* is an ancestor and call it ancestor worship. They say that your grandmother or grandfather comes to you every now and then to tell you what is going to happen and what to do and what not to do. And there is a lot of literature on the subject now that refers to *aumakua* as guardian spirit or guardian angel.

Now in a way I guess that a guardian angel would be a ghost. Sometimes the *aumakua* may take the form of various animals—a shark or bird, a *pueo* (Hawaiian owl), for instance—and we speak of a particular bird with a particular name or a particular shark with a particular name or even a particular legend that has a particular name, the *mo'o.*

And all of these things give the idea of the American Indians and the Australian aboriginal concept of the totem. In a way these animal forms point to reincarnation or living forms of ancestors and the *aumakua* is the animal itself.

I just finished reading a Ph.D. thesis by a woman in San Diego who was comparing the work of Max Freedom Long with David "Daddy" Bray. She wrote that Bray went from the point of view of the Polynesians to the point of view of the westerner and Max went from the point of view of the westerner to the point of view of the Polynesians, as he understood it.

When anyone is writing, they are writing about phenomena as they understand it, as they read about it, or how they were told. So all that you write and I write are the results of our total experience. According to Max Freedom Long, who speaks of the subconscious or the *umipili* (the mind that never forgets), we are able to dredge up those experiences through dreams or meditation. Yet when we come to it, a dream is involuntary and meditation is voluntary, so when we are concentrating we are attempting to call up a previous experience. Max refers to a dream as *moi uhane*, which refers to the consciousness of sleep or the spirit in sleep. Sleep is actually the subconscious and not a conscious thing.

Serge King has written quite a bit also and not only talks about his experiences but those of his father as well. His father fell in a hole in the ground one day and was then rescued. While he was in the hole, he became a *kahuna* and henceforth wrote voluminous material from his own viewpoint. And all those things are ghosts in a way.

I worked with Max Freedom Long for two years. I lived in Hollywood for a year and then in Westwood, California. Max lived in Hollywood as well so we got together often. All in all, I was in contact with Max when he was alive for twenty-three years. We had a voluminous correspondence over those years. He would publish bulletins every two weeks that went all over the world. Foreigners would write to him of their experiences and he would incorporate them in the books he wrote. He wrote seven books and I have all of them autographed by Max Freedom Long. His teachings are a sound basis for the study of *huna* today.

People in the east are closer to their primitive lives and so are more unified but in America, and Hawaii especially, our unity is gone so that even in ghost stories today we are influenced by different racial groups that have come in to our picture so they are not true Hawaiian ghost stories anymore, but much influenced by these other people and their ancestors. So now we have ancestor worship, which is a ghost. Any form of worship is a ghost. From the Buddhist point of view the word Buddha means enlightenment and the word Christ or Christ-light comes from the Greek word *crispus* so from that concept, Christ is a ghost! In the Christian religion, it is the Holy Ghost as is the Buddha as well.

A ghost can be positive or negative. The Chinese refer to Yin and Yang and the Hawaiians refer to Ku and Hina. Ku would be Yang and Hina would be Yin. Yang would be male or positive force and Yin would be female or negative, receptive vibration, the eternal dualities that make up the universe. Every one of us is part male and part female. According to early anthropologists, at one time the world was matrilineal, the Po period, originally coming from the mother. Today everything comes from the father. It is patrilineal. The government is patriarchal when at one time it was matriarchal. When we pray to God we pray to Our Father. In India they still often pray to Divine Mother because they are closer to their primitive world, closer to the source. The more you have western influence, the further away you get from the source. When the western viewpoint comes into the picture, it disrupts the source. There is a Ku in every person and a Hina in every person, both halves that form the whole. Ku means upright, vertical, or longitudinal. Hina is latitudinal. Wherever you go you need both longitude and latitude to describe your particular location.

If you delve into it, you will find that the basic philosophy of the ancient *kahuna* was very deep without the various elements that have come into the picture. The more of the various racial groups that come to Hawaii, the more distortion takes place. You have some groups like the Japanese who try very hard to remain within themselves. They try only to marry within themselves. The English are mixed. For example, King George was a German who died without speaking English and today's queen is married to a Greek. In America, it's a hodgepodge. In other groups of people, their ghosts are subjective, but when you come to Americans or even people in Hawaii, their ghosts are objective, modern, technical, as is the culture. Even their ghosts are a mixture now. At this present time it is impossible to bring about unity so long as we have the kind of culture we have."

"The thing is, Mr. Kenn," I broke in, "the world has come to a point today in the 1980s and from now on that all of the boundaries—racial, national, geographical and all—are blurring due to increased communication and the world's having grown so small that we are being forced into a consciousness of being a global people rather than being able to concentrate—as you pointed out regarding the people of Japan—on their unity. We still do that to an extent of course, but we now have to expand at the same time to be able to accept the rest of the world on an equal footing because we have no other choice."

"But in the United States at least," Mr. Kenn retorted, "to my point of view at this present time, it is impossible to bring about unity in so long as you have the form of government that we have."

"I agree!" I responded. "I think you just put your finger on it. That's why in order to come to any sort of understanding, we are going to have to go beyond government restrictions and we are going to have to come together through a spiritual understanding—or viewpoint. That is exactly why I think this work is important! Because it provides a foundation for people to be able to exchange information and experiences on a *universal* level aside from cultural, religious, philosophical or..."

"Economic?" interjected Mr. Kenn.

"That's right," I said, "economic and racial divisions. Everyone is being pushed apart economically. That's a huge situation today because of misunderstandings through governments and politics within a given country, much less overseas. But if we can at least come together in a small way, it is one little step towards an international bridge of understanding where people can share what is really important—our universal experience of life itself—which comes through pure sources like the Hawaiian people. We are reaching a point where we cannot continue to maintain the racial identities anymore to the point of division. Hawaii is just one perfect example of racial harmony, for the most part. Singapore reminded me of Hawaii as a melting pot as people come there from all over the world. There are East Indians, Malaysians, Chinese, and Indonesians everybody compelled to blend together on a day-to-day basis, cultural boundaries blurring, teaching each other, and sharing. So if we preserve what is precious and pure and, at the same time, share that with other people, then at least it is a start towards brotherhood and peace. But it has to be a spiritual blending. It's not going to happen any other way. As you pointed out, we are all yin and yang, *ku* and *hina*. We all come from the same source. We are all one."

We paused for a moment as a new understanding began to dawn.

Finally Mr. Kenn cleared his throat and said, "Yes. Now in your study of ghosts and in your forthcoming book, as you see it, what could be the final result? Dissemination of information?"

"No," I replied rather firmly, surprising even myself. "I would hope for a better mutual understanding of people coming from different points of view, from different windows of experience as it were as you said, coming together through different doorways to form a universal basis for wholeness and balance through understanding of our shared experiences. To realize that all differences are superficial and that at core we are all alike. We are all the same, no matter what language we speak or what part of the globe we inhabit, what culture has formed us, or what religion or philosophy we believe or adhere to. For example, on a limited basis, you know the stories I collected here in Hawaii on the Chokeneck phenomena. Well, I flew to Malaysia, got off the plane in Kuala Lumpur and my friend picked me up via taxi. On the way back to the apartment, they told me that the apartment was experiencing a ghost. The landlady, a Moslem woman, had a recent experience that sounded identical to Chokeneck in every detail. Later it was known that a man had died in her apartment a year before. His body lay undiscovered for three days in the same bed that she was using. She described the pressure on her throat and chest, the paralysis, the whole thing. She struggled for several minutes before she was able to throw it off by reciting in her mind a verse from the Koran. Immediately it was released and she was free of it. Many of the Chokeneck stories I collected were similar. One man was Catholic and made the sign of the cross with the tip of his little finger and that released it. A Japanese fireman recited a Buddhist sutra in his head and that released it. A schoolteacher in Waianae mentally said her Hawaiian protection chant and that released it from her. So you see whatever the religious background, training or belief, it was apparently coming from the same source and this particular phenomenon was dissipated by people reaching into their own belief system using whatever religious tools they had and the results were exactly the same. This in itself provides a kind of universal bridge of understanding."

"People are always going to have differences. They are always going to be separate—as it should be as this is the beauty of it. It's like a garden full of flowers. You don't want all of the flowers to be the same! The beauty is in the variety of blossoms so you may appreciate the unique qualities of each flower while enjoying the grandeur of the entire garden blooming in harmony. So those are the results I would hope to come from this work."

"In regards to ghosts," said Mr. Kenn, "do you recognize what we call Christian ghosts or Buddhist ghosts?"

"Are you talking about apparitions?" I replied. "A spiritual apparition that appears?"

"Yes," he said. "Uh huh. In Siam (Thailand) for example, or in the East Indies, are there ghosts based upon the Buddha or his prophets when in the west, would we have Christian or Polynesian ghosts? Are there such things?"

"Ah, you see," I sighed, "that is the keynote to all of this. The ghosts all seem to be the same. They seem to take the same forms no matter what the background of the people. And the people who are not expecting to see or experience these things (and in many cases do not believe in any of it) go ahead and experience it anyway!

"So what casts it off then depends on the person's religious training or belief system?"

"That's right," I said, "and the result seems to be the same no matter what the beliefs are. That's the interesting part of this and without coming to any conclusions but by just looking at what's happening, I've observed that people are telling me the truth of their own experience. They are not sitting there making up a story. They are not lying about it. They are sharing their own reality and experience."

Mr. Kenn smiled and a glint came into his eyes when he said, "Isn't the concept of a ghost a lie?"

"Meaning the concept of something that does not exist or something unreal?" I retorted.

"Yes," he grinned.

"But hasn't it been said that life itself is a dream and something that, in essence, is unreal?" I retorted.

"Yes, that's true."

"So who's to say?" I shrugged. "I don't think that any one person or any religion has the final answer. Truth is truth. People discover their own answers and construct their own beliefs. If you can see that certain things seem to hold true no matter where or when or how they come, then I think this gives a basis for hope."

"Would you say," Mr. Kenn baited, "that God Himself is a ghost?"

"You mean in that he does not physically exist?"

"In that he exists in your mind. He exists for you and for you only," he said.

"You could say that I suppose. Yes, I think so... among other things!" I smiled. "Could *you* say that God is a ghost?"

"I think so, yes," he replied thoughtfully, "and ghosts in the sense from one point of view that a ghost is superstition and supernatural and from another viewpoint that it is real."

"If you talk to people who have experienced them," I exclaimed, "they will tell you in no uncertain terms they are real!"

Mr. Kenn smiled his approval. "Your mind is a ghost. As the Buddha said, 'Man's mind is God.' Dr. Buck says, 'First man creates God and then God turns around and creates man.'"

"Oh, I like that," I agreed, "It's almost a zen koan. You can think about that one around and around and around..."

"So a ghost is also a belief, a faith and not necessarily that seeing is believing, but thinking is believing and dreaming is believing. Jesus is a ghost. The so-called *akua* is a ghost. We believe in ghosts. We depend upon ghosts for our very being. Magic—what we call positive and negative magic or black and white—are ghosts. It is what we think. Our mind is a ghost. Our ghosts exist out of sight, out of mind. Our ghosts exist because we believe in them. So if you ask a thousand people for their definition of ghost, you will find as many definitions as there are people and yet a ghost would probably be the sum of all those things put together. As you just said, God is the sum of what all people put together think while looking at him through different windows."

"Which is the way it should be," I nodded. "Which is beautiful, don't you think?"

"Yes, in a way," he agreed reluctantly, "if people understand that instead of saying my God is more powerful than your God."

"Or my window is the only window!" I agreed.

"And that's what the missionaries taught the Hawaiians," he frowned, "that their Christian god was more powerful than the Hawaiian god and yet the Hawaiians never had gods! Today in one of your states (South Dakota) you have the likenesses of different U.S. presidents carved into a mountain. Idols, hm? If you refer to the pictures of Jesus made during the Renaissance and pictures of Jesus today, you see two different people. And yet no artist ever saw Jesus Himself."

"So Jesus is an idol," he continued, "and an idol is a ghost, but man needs that. Man needs to believe. Man needs to have faith and that is why there are so many different churches and so many different points of view. Yet you say they are all the same. You say that your God and my God are the same God."

"A woman once told me a story. She went to a funeral at a Chinese cemetery and she saw food all spread out in front of the graves. The woman asked one of the men, 'When do you expect your dead to eat that?' and the man answered her, 'When your dead smell the flowers you put on their graves.'"

Charles Kenn sighed. "Father, Son, Holy Ghost, Amen. People say that as a ritual. Hawaiians say *Makua, Keiki, Himulele, Amene*. We refer to the Holy Spirit and some people say, the Holy Ghost. When they say Holy Ghost it means in their minds. There is such a thing as an unholy ghost."

"By deduction, yes," I submitted.

"So what is the unholy ghost?" Mr. Kenn was revving up again. "It is the ghost the other person believes in while the Holy Ghost is the ghost that I believe in! I believe in the Holy Ghost and my adversary believes in the unholy ghost or the devil or St. Lucifer. Take your pick. According to the Bible, St. Lucifer was a twin of Jesus who was cast out. The Bible is a book for sinners. The Bible is a black book."

"Ooooh," I gasped, "that could be argued!"

But Mr. Kenn continued, both energized and unfazed. "A ghost is a ghost! To some people a ghost is holy and by inference a ghost is also unholy or evil. So we have good ghosts and bad ghosts, as there is positive and negative. Yet people always say we believe in the positive and we reject the negative. And yet we cannot live without the negative. Yang cannot exist without yin. *Ku* cannot exist without *hina*."

"Black cannot exist without white," I said completing his thought. Rather a powerful thought, I mused.

He gave me a sharp look.

"After you have gathered up all your material and your book is completed," he said seriously, "it will have a great influence on a lot of people who read it. It will probably set a pace affecting the thoughts of people who have never before had those concepts of what a ghost is and many will be confused, but they will start thinking."

"And that is good," I said, smiling my thanks for his encouragement. He smiled in return.

"One more point," he said. "Westervelt refers to 'ghost-gods,' hyphenated yet one word. The point is this: all gods are ghosts."

"But not all ghosts are gods," I replied.

There was nothing more to say.

Judi Thompson prepares to board the small plane to Kalaupapa, Molokai.